The Myths and Mysteries
of Marriage

❖

The Myths and Mysteries of Marriage

Making relationships work

Roland Trujillo

This book is dedicated to all the men and women everywhere who stay together, for richer or for poorer, for better or worse, until death do them part.

CONTENTS

- 1 -

The Dating and Mating Game Is Not a Game

Relationships make the world go around. We love people and we hate them. We want to be around them and then we want to get away from them. We can't live with them, and we can't live without them.

And nowhere is this more evident than when it comes to dating, courtship, long term and short term relationships, partners and spouses.

First I want to say that all relationships start off with excitement and dreams of living happily ever after, and yet a large percentage end up as a living hell. Many of us saw our parents arguing and fighting and we hated it.

We were sure that our relationship would be different. But once we got involved with someone for awhile--sure enough, soon we were arguing—and we are lucky if it was merely arguing. Sad to say the daily newspapers are full of stories about arguments that turn into violence or even murder.

Something is wrong. If love turns into hatred, then it wasn't real love to start with. It proves that what most people think of as love is not really love at all.

Some relationships settle into long ones. Many appear happy and fulfilling on the surface. But the truth is that many are not. Something is still wrong. Each partner suffers--he in his way, and she in her way.

I remember when I was a boy, my mother had some good lady friends. I was surprised and shocked by what was said about their husbands. Each wife not only openly complained about and criticized her husband, but also stated that she was secretly unhappy and unfulfilled.

I was shocked because in private they seemed to have contempt for their husbands, and what was said in private was quite different than what was said when the husbands were present.

I also got to listen in to what the husbands said when, for example, the men would go fishing while the women did something else.

When I was with men, I heard a different story. The men were unaware of their wife's secret unhappiness or of their wife's secret contempt. The husbands thought that everything was basically okay with the marriage.

The men did admit that their wives never seemed to be satisfied. The wives always wanted something. They wanted him to lose weight, to stop smoking, get a better job (like some other friend's husband had), or go to church more. The wife wanted him to improve or change in some way.

The wives, according to the husbands, were apparently never satisfied. They wanted a bigger house, more furniture, a vacation, or something. But when she got it, she was still not satisfied with it. Nor was she satisfied with any self improvement he made. She always found something to disapprove of. Yet the husbands were not aware of their wife's secret unhappiness or that the wife was complaining about him behind his back.

The husband typically said that his wife was confusing, and he was at a loss as to what she wanted.

But like I said, for the most part, the men thought that the relationship was basically okay. Without trying to be rude, I must say (to use an old expression) the men were "fat, dumb and happy." They did not suspect the deep unhappiness their wives were feeling.

Occasionally one of the husbands or wives would privately remark that they were staying together "for the sake of the kids."

It seemed as though the wives were far unhappier with the husbands than vice versa. Somehow they wanted something from their husbands that they were not getting. The wives seemed to think that what was needed was better communication, intimacy and sharing that would make things right.

But their unhappiness and continued complaints no matter what their husband did proves that it was something deeper that they needed.

They could not put into words what they needed. But I can. And I will spell it out in this book.

Their husbands could not figure out what their partners wanted. They tried everything--from flowers to champagne and hot tubs for two—but nothing seemed to satisfy the wives.

I will tell you husbands later what they want, so keep reading.

- 2 -

"A Rose by Any Other Name is Still a Rose"

Before continuing, I want those of you who are not married but are living together to pardon my frequent use of the terms "husband and wife." That's the way it was back then when I was a kid observing mom and dad and their friends. Things really were like the television shows *Father Knows Best* or *Leave it to Beaver*. For one thing—everyone was married.

Things are a little different now. So I want to be more inclusive, and that is why you will see the term "relationships" and "partners" more frequently in this book than in my previous book.

Nevertheless, I still have to say that the formality of the marriage vows--binding two people together spiritually, emotionally, and civilly, with that commitment being made public and permanent for all to see--is still the gold standard.

Let's face it—if you really love someone, you want them to be committed and loyal to you permanently not temporarily. How do you feel if you find out your boy friend is dating someone else, or your girl friend is seeing someone else? What do you think of a husband who puts his wedding ring in his pocket when he is around someone interesting?

A permanent bond is what we want, at least at first.

When our "love" (which was not really love) turns to hate, we may then look for escape. But what do most of us do? We "escape" into another relationship (which we hope will give us the permanent fulfillment we crave).

Therefore, in this book I will use the term "marriage" to indicate a permanent loving bond.

But whether you call yours a marriage or a long term relationship, or whether you had it formalized or not, I will not quibble over terminology. This book is about love and about making relationships work, not about what you call them. This book is for everyone--married or not. So whether you are in a long term relationship, married, betrothed, getting into a relationship, just getting over one, or not in any relationship but are curious about the topic—welcome!

Later in the book I may address why, in the long run, a formal marriage arrangement provides emotional security for the woman and why it is a thing of honor that the man would be wise to consider. But for now, I just want those of you who are living together to understand that I'm not going to condemn you for it.

What is in the heart is more important than a piece of paper. I believe that in the long run, a formalized arrangement is good for the two of you, but if you see it differently, I respect your opinion and don't want to argue. Some of you are not yet sure about what to do, and might consider marriage if you thought it would be helpful. That's fair enough. Later in the book I will give you my side of the argument for your consideration.

But no matter what you call it, a relationship is a bond and there will be a bonding process involved. I can tell you right now that there is no such thing as just hooking up. You always take something from the other and give something. A little bit of them gets into you and vice versa. That is why promiscuity is destructive of character. And that is also why one man and one woman forever is a very positive thing.

Perhaps now you can see why something so powerful and potentially beautiful is fraught with danger and trouble if not handled properly.

Here's an analogy. When a chemist at a laboratory mixes chemicals together, he has to be careful and follow rules and procedures. Otherwise the whole thing could explode in his face.

When it comes to the joining together of two people, which involves not only physical union but also spiritual and, as we have seen, identity exchange—there must be rules and principles involved. These rules and principles would be for the protection of the people involved. The chemist in the laboratory does not think that the instructions and procedures are meant to restrict him. He knows they are meant to help and protect him.

Therefore, I am here to suggest that relationships, being a far more volatile combination than any chemical one, must have principles that govern the union in order to protect and vouchsafe a successful union.

And if what I have said is true, then a prudent woman or man would seek to determine what those principles are.

But what do most of us do? We jump into relationships with abandon. We take more care in buying a car then we do in choosing who we will bond with. And once we are in a relationship and things start to go wrong, we seem to be incapable of preventing them from getting worse and worse.

The latter is particularly troubling because despite our folly, many of us do manage to marry someone decent.

It is sad to see two basically good people, who are trying to make their marriage work, nevertheless get in trouble and don't know how to make things right.

Granted, sometimes getting older and wiser and basically growing up and maturing have a mellowing effect on people. A couple might fight like cats and dogs when they are young, but if they stay together long enough, the softening and chastening effect of life may help them to mellow and begin to appreciate each other.

However before we get too sentimental, it is also the case that many if not most long term marriages are also lives of secret unhappiness, unfinished business and hidden resentments. Often one side clams up and becomes suppressed; the other becomes dominant (and perhaps cruel). Sometimes both live separate lives, throwing themselves into work or community activities.

Don't get me wrong—there is nothing wrong with commitment to work or community. In fact, I think a good deal of separation—whether it's separate beds or separate work activities—helps prevent unwholesome closeness of the sticky enmeshing kind that makes you feel trapped. When both people are separately involved in wholesome productive activities, whether at home or the workplace, and both are growing and leading fulfilling lives, it is healthier and more liberating environment than being too close.

What I am saying is that buried hostility, hidden resentments, unfinished business, secret judgments and contempt, and undercurrents of anger are what ruin many marriages that appear made in heaven to the untrained observer.

But the kids know. Kids are very perceptive. They can tell when dad is angry underneath, and they sense mom's resentment and contempt for dad. They pick up on the secret unhappiness, and it troubles them and makes them unhappy too.

The other problem is that, as bad as marital resentment can be, divorce is usually even worse for the kids.

The biggest harm of broken relationships is the effect on the kids. Societal and financial ruin pale in comparison to the devastation of divorce on the kids.

Obviously I am talking about two basically decent people. If one of the partners is a drug addict, violent, a criminal or an abuser, then separation from such a person is usually prudent to protect the safety of the children.

But like I said, I have seen too many basically decent people who have built a life and a family together divorce over minor misunderstandings and a build up of resentment.

Sometimes they just hope to improve their relationship but then fall into the hands of some marriage and family therapist who makes things worse or even encourages divorce.

Divorce is not the answer to squabbling or marital unhappiness. Some couples think it would be better to divorce so that the kids won't see them arguing. Kids would rather see mom and dad squabbling than separating.

Why divorce is so hurtful to the kids I will leave for you to discover as you read this book.

Perhaps the basic theme of what I have been saying should be stated as a way of introducing the rest of the book. It is this. Marriage is more than two animals copulating, and it is more than just a living arrangement for the convenience of two selfish egos. It is physical, emotional, communal, and above spiritual. Humans have souls. A marriage is the coming together of two souls.

- 3 -

Why I Decided to Become a Pastor

If the Creator made laws to govern nature, then He must have also made rules to govern human conduct.

And He must have made principles concerning the union and bonding of human beings. It says somewhere in the Bible that "what is seen is made by what is unseen." The principles are spiritual, and not observable. But the results of violating or ignoring them are very observable. Just look at the devastation and unhappiness all around us.

None of us starts out wanting to violate delicate principles to ruin our relationship. We all start off with the hope of happiness. But what has happened is that we are unaware of the principles.

We are ignorant of them because we have been mis-educated and kept in the dark.

Our leaders and educators, those who are supposed to know, are also often woefully unaware or themselves mis-educated about what makes relationships work.

Those around us--such as our parents, colleagues, friends, and the so called experts--are also often ignorant of important principles. Some of them are even in denial about God and about the fact that humans have souls.

For example, if an educator, college instructor, writer or counselor thinks that we are just evolved apes, that sex is just two animals copulating, and that marriage is a mere social convention—how can he or she possibly teach or project a spiritual approach to marriage?

Fortunately, many ministers and church people still generally say the right things. They talk about moral principles, purity, abstinence, waiting until marriage to consummate the marriage, and about avoiding divorce.

Though some of them waiver in order to be popular or politically correct, nevertheless they have the Scriptures and a tradition of moral living and family values which they usually refer to.

I have to say that much of their advice about pre-marriage—dating, courtship and engagement--is generally quite good. For example, they talk about the dangers of causal dating and the devastation of promiscuous sex. They point out the benefits of purity, of abstinence and of waiting until marriage.

Some churches also have some excellent pre marriage workshops and seminars that help young couples think about marriage, about really getting to know the other person before getting too involved, and about carefully determining what your values and the other person's values really are before taking the big step of getting married.

As good and helpful as these messages could be, the church has two things working against it. First, the secular popular culture teaches just the opposite by word, deed, and implication. Don't forget that among Christians, over 90% send their kids to secular public schools. Then when their kids take drugs, have promiscuous sex, and become worldly, the parents scratch their heads and can't figure out what went wrong. They don't get it.

If you, as a parent, transfer your authority to someone else who operates in a secular institution that forbids teaching religious values, and if you leave your kids there 5 days a week 7 hours a day, for 12 years--then what do you expect?

Don't get me wrong, I'm not saying that there are not some decent moral teachers in public schools, nor am I suggesting that kids be indoctrinated with Christianity, or for that matter Communism, Darwinism, socialism, or any other ism.

What I am saying is that the secular culture is at best somewhat confusing and amoral, and generally tends to be anti religious in its orientation. That's just the way it is.

The other thing that the church has working against it is the types of people whose rhetoric and rigidity give Christianity a bad name. The old fashioned hell fire and brimstone style preachers try to scare people and play upon their fears. These types do more harm than good.

Though they may even be saying the right things, their rigidity, their self righteousness and unfortunately, their hypocrisy make them despicable and not credible.

But lest you think I am picking on the church or the clergy, I wish to remind you that I am an ordained minister. My hope is that I can speak the truth without wavering, with firm conviction but in humility and without emotionalism. My hope is that my writings will help awaken you, so that you can see for yourself what is true. I do not wish to push any dogma on you. My goal is to awaken you to realize. By talking about spiritual principles, I may remind you of them, and perhaps my words will help you to see that they do exist and that they might be of help to you.

I also don't want people to put me on a pedestal, nor do I want them to accept what I say because I have a title or degree.

For over twenty years I spoke and wrote without reference to title or degree. Although I already had a couple of degrees, I did not mention them. If anything I say is true, it should be self evident, and it should conform to what you see intuitively is right. It should conform to common sense. If it is true, it is not because I say so or because I have a title or degree, but because it is so.

Therefore I wanted to avoid someone believing something I said because of "the white coat syndrome."

The while coat syndrome refers to the fact that many people will believe what some someone says because they are influenced by a white coat and a stethoscope around the neck.

If I had on clergy clothes and a couple of degrees framed on the wall, some people would be hypnotized by the clothes and the degrees. They would accept what I said mindlessly, not because they see for themselves but because they are influenced by the religious garb and degree on the wall.

On the other hand, many people (far more than you would suspect) who have had bad experiences with religious types, would have an aversion and react against me because of their prior negative experiences with religious authorities. They would react emotionally against the title of pastor even though I am nothing like the religious types they knew before. This would make it difficult or impossible to hear the message I bring because their emotional reaction would get in the way.

These people have come in contact with wicked and hypocritical people who hid behind religion or some other title in order to pressure and confuse others.

In fact, Satan sometimes does his greatest damage by having his agents in the church. These wolves in sheep's clothing do much harm and cause decent people to develop an aversion or even a hatred of religion.

So I remained a layperson and simply wrote and talked about some of the things that I see. I have never pressured anyone to believe or accept me or what I say.

However, I began to see that many people do look to the clergy for some sort of guidance. When they get into a tight spot, they would like to talk to a pastor.

I also began to see how woefully and pitifully weak the clergy sometimes is when it comes to helping with the mental health, emotional, and relationship issues that people are dealing with in real life.

For example, when it comes to helping with such issues as: depression, anxiety, and stress, I also saw how weak most clergy and Christian counselors are when it comes to the reliance on psychiatric meds.

Many of them simply buy into the biomedical model, the so-called "chemical imbalance" in the brain theory.

They read it somewhere or saw it in a pharmaceutical ad.

Those who aren't sure nevertheless take a back seat to psychiatrists or psychologists. The once queen of science, theology, plays second fiddle to the Godless pseudoscience of psychiatry.

Many clergy and ambitious Christians study psychology and get degrees so as to fit into the system, get positions of power, and lord it over others with the pompous jargon of the day. They study and then actually spout the flavor of the day theory and confuse and betray their parishioners or those who seek their help by selling them out.

Others strongly suspect that the chemical theory is not based in solid science, but they remain mute out of fear of being politically incorrect or being labeled as old fashioned.

I will never forget what a caring advocate, who helps returning soldiers and veterans, said. In lamenting the multiple psychiatric meds that troubled soldiers are routinely put on, he said "you cannot medicate a moral dilemma or ethical crisis away."

The phrase "you cannot medicate a moral dilemma away" made me take note. Many of our soldiers have seen things in battle that no one should have to witness.

Many of them have been betrayed, used, lied to, and asked to do things that they begin to question the morality of. In short they are troubled by what they did and troubled by what they saw.

They are troubled in the spirit and are doing some soul searching. They need thoughtful guidance, wise counsel, and time to work through some of the issues they are pondering deeply. Instead they are given a diagnosis and almost always prescribed psychiatric meds, and more often than not, multiple ones. I, like the caring advocate I heard, see something wrong with this.

How sad it is when these troubled souls are sold out by the spiritual caregivers they hoped would have spiritual, moral and ethical answers for them.

I came to see that a shocking percentage of those in the church who give advice are themselves weak, misguided and confused.

I decided that becoming a pastor might help in making me available to those who might be looking for spiritual answers.

At least it would give me a platform so that some people might lend me their ear. Then they might be gratified to hear someone with understanding of basic human spiritual needs. I also reasoned that an advanced degree in psychology would bring me up to date on the latest theories and totally familiar with terminology and current practices so I could relate better to what people who seek my help have been told about their issue and what type of help they have been receiving.

That, in a nutshell, is how I came about deciding to become a pastor.

It is my fervent hope that I will be the type of person who properly represents true Christianity. If I speak from the heart, present the message in a credible way, seek to awaken people rather than pressure them, and tell them the truth instead of selling them out or offering false reassurances—I might help some people who give me their ear because of my credentials, but then they get the real message and have their faith in what they know in their heart restored.

- *4* -

Where to Find Real Solutions to your Relationship Woes

I also wish to say that it is too easy to blame the church or the schools. When things go wrong at home, such as when the kids start going astray, parents often take two approaches: First they look to someone else to solve their problems, such as the schools, the government or organized religion. Then when things go even more wrong, they blame the ones who they went to, and then again, demand that the outside institution do even more. Blaming is a distraction from seeing the part that they played in what went wrong. Looking to someone else to solve your problems breeds dependency and stifles real growth.

I will elaborate on the above themes.

Parents, for example, often blame the church, the schools, the popular culture, or the government. They fix blame on an institution, as if it were the school's fault that the kids have gone astray. But I have to say that the number one influence on the kids is still the parents. If others begin to have too much influence on the kids, it is because of the default of parents who have abdicated their authority and handed over the kids to someone else.

And when it comes to marriage, the Moses of the family and the person to whom the wife should look up to with respect is the husband. If he is weak, violent, uninformed, or if he makes her his god, then how can she respect him?

If he does not have wisdom, how can the family look to him to guide them when things get a little rough?

And if he does not have the faith and conviction to do what is right and wise, because he is too deferential to what others say, how can he keep the family from being misled?

Another variation of the "blame the schools and the government card" is blaming the economy. "If the economy were better and if we only had more money, we wouldn't have to argue. We could live in a better neighborhood, have more things, pay our bills, and have a better house. Then the marriage would be better. If the schools had more money for computers, then the kids would excel."

I hope you realize that none of the above is true. People can be happy with very little. As the old saying goes, "The best things in life are not things." Abraham Lincoln educated himself using the fireplace for light, and with only one book!

I also want to put in a word of defense for the churches. I have already said that wolves in sheep's clothing have gotten into the church and are very wicked, leading many people astray and turning others off to the very thing that could help them.

But having said that, I must also say in defense of the churches and the ministers—many church people are decent and do good work. Please don't tell me about the inquisition. I know that a great deal of harm has been done in the guise of religion. I already said that twice in this book. But I also know that when there's an earthquake in Haiti or a typhoon in Indonesia, the ones who always arrive with medical help, supplies and food are the Christian churches.

I also know in my heart that many of the Christian people who are my neighbors, friends, and associates are good people.

If they have any fault it is that they are a bit gullible and authority oriented. They are too trusting of the powers that be, and they believe more in various authorities' nice clever words than in what they know in their heart. Being too trusting is probably why over 90% of Christian parents march their kids off to the public schools, which now have American students ranking below third world countries in academic achievement.

Being too authority oriented, they look to the government to do something, to the church leaders to teach them and tell them what is right, and to science and medicine to save them from their unhealthy lifestyles.

When we put others on a pedestal, believe and trust in everything they say, and look to them to do for us— this puts a huge and unfair burden on the authorities.

They try harder and harder to help, cure, and save us from our own folly. But they are only human.

And before long, our weakness tempts them to have contempt for us or to take advantage of our naiveté.

Intuition and true religion

The Good Lord gave us intuition—old fashioned common sense. We have forgotten our own American heritage. We have forgotten Ralph Waldo Emerson, Theodore Roosevelt, Thomas Edison, and the pioneers.

These people—in everyday matters, in politics and in morality—followed and trusted what they saw for themselves. They followed common sense, they lived intuitively, and that's why they became pioneers, inventors, and free spirits.

We have forgotten that people like Abraham, Enoch, Elijah, Ruth and the prophets did not go to church.

They did not look to some organization or some religious expert to tell them about religion. It was truly one person and his or her God.

Most people do not know where to find God. He is within. And the way to know religion is not through some go-between middle man. Nor is from studying some words in a book.

The way to know God is to experience Him. The way to know truth is to realize it.

And you are never closer to beginning to experience the touch of God then when you realize something through wordless intuition. God sends His Light, and your soul realizes Truth in this Light. It is a wordless way of knowing. It is knowing without words.

Realizing is like seeing. Another term for realizing is intuition. Some people call it a wordless hunch, sixth sense, or a gut level knowing. Our biggest problem is doubt. We doubt the inner wordless testimony. We believe more in what others say than in what we know in our hearts.

We also forget what God said in the Bible:

"I will put my laws into their mind, and write them in their hearts: and I will be to them a God, and they shall be to me a people.

And they shall not teach every man his neighbor, and every man his brother, saying, Know the Lord:

For all shall know me, from the least to the greatest."
Hebrews 8, verses 10, 11 KJV

God wants us to live intuitively. He wants us to use our intuition and common sense. That's why He gave us intuition. What the ancient prophets called living by faith is living intuitively. God does not want us to follow hypocrites or Pharisees. Nor does he want us to mindlessly accept what someone says. He wants us to see it for ourselves.

At one point, Christ said to Peter: "who do you say that I am?" Peter answered: "You are the Christ, the Son of the Living God".

Then Christ said a very interesting thing. He said: "Blessed art thou, Simon Peter, for flesh and blood have not revealed this to you, but my Father in Heaven."

No one told Peter who Christ was. Peter knew it wordlessly. It was revealed to him within.

We all have access to this type of knowing, which is far superior to mere intellectual knowledge. But we disregard it and ignore it. And of course we doubt it.

When it comes to finances, to raising our kids, to relating to our partner, and to discovering the reason for our existence—we must learn to trust the wordless Word within. When you desire to know the truth and you wish with all your heart to do the right thing but don't know what the right thing is, your true need and pure intent will stress the Spirit. All of a sudden you will see what do.

And when you trust that wordless knowing and act on it, then you will marvel at how problems resolve themselves, as if by magic. Without effort on your part.

We must all learn to go into our room and practice becoming still, so that we might find our intuition and learn to relate to it. We must learn to pay attention to what it is quietly trying to tell us, so that we can realize what is right, fair and just. We must live by common sense and intuition. We must wait until we know, without words, what to do.

Waiting for guidance from within, and in all matters no matter how small, checking with conscience (intuition)—this I believe is what is meant in the Bible by Paul's instruction to pray without ceasing.

That is why packaged programs about saving your marriage, about disciplining your kids, or losing weight are bound to fail. They are externally based, and not intuitive.

That is why clever pre planned answers fail.

When your child is standing in front of you with an issue, s/he can tell whether you are speaking spontaneously from the heart or whether you are smoothly regurgitating something you heard or read.

When you speak something preplanned, the life and love is taken out of it.

When some issue arises with your spouse, there are not enough books in the world to guide you through the subtlety of the moment. What you need in that important moment is just in time guidance. You need what the French call le mot juste (just the right word).

You need savoir faire (intuitive know how), a delicate sense of timing, and you need to get your ego out of the way. You need patience. You need guidance from your Creator. That is what intuition is for.

This point is spoken to in the Bible when Christ says: when you are called before the authorities, do not plan what to say in advance, the Holy Spirit will guide you.

Elsewhere in this book I relate how a wife who had some marital issues went to a counselor.

This wife's husband was decent, a good provider, not a womanizer or drinker. Just a decent guy. But she and he had some issues, like many couples do. The counselor cavalierly encouraged her to divorce and "do her own thing." The marriage was destroyed, the kids suffered and both husband and wife lived out their separate lives in sickness and in poverty.

The counselor, a recent graduate who had little experience and no understanding, was a fool. But I am not going to blame the counselor.

The real problem was that this lady's husband was typical of husbands: he was decent but weak and unaware. She resented him, and soon her resentment ruined her emotional well being and made her judgmental over everything he did.

He did not see or understand what was going on. He could not understand why she was unhappy. He did not know what else was required of him. He did not have the agape love she needed from him. Nor was he aware enough to protect her from unwholesome influences or see the problem with the foolish advice she was getting from strangers.

No one had loved him either. No one had taken the time to guide him properly. He was a victim. And then through his weakness, she became a victim too. But I'm not making excuses to him. Because of his failing, the whole family suffered.

If we had been left without help, and the human race had been left to fend for itself, then it would be unfair.

But we were not left unattended. At this very moment, as you read this book, you have access to guidance from within. But chances are you do not even know that you have it or how to find it and interpret what it is trying to wordlessly tell you. If you believe in intuition at all, you probably think it is just women who have a woman's intuition.

Thus when issues arise that you need wisdom to deal with, you turn your back on intuition, and you look to experts, teachers, and strangers.

Of course, the lady I was telling you about could have been reasonably happy if she could have learned to give up resentment and judgment. Her resentment was hurting her more than anything else.

She could have paid attention to and believed her intuition (conscience) which was telling her to not resent and judge her husband.

No one reminded her of this. And if they did, they didn't have the love to speak directly and make their words crystal clear so she couldn't duck the message. Nor could they tell her the why and how of giving up resentment.

If she had heard the warning, it would have awakened her to her inner intuition (conscience) which had been telling her wordlessly all along--to not resent her husband.

Nevertheless, even if someone had made it crystal clear, she would probably have been unwilling to give up the resentment. Like many people, she was too stubborn to admit she was wrong.

Judging and resenting her husband gave her a sense of self righteousness, and she felt like a martyr. It gave her someone to hate, to blame and to have contempt for. Resentment ultimately robbed her of happiness, family, and then perhaps her soul.

But what if this lady had been one of the rare souls (which hopefully you may be too) who when the truth is stated clearly and with love, she sees herself in its light and is sorry for what she sees? Repenting of her resentment and judgment, her soul softens as she awakens to the Creator's love within. Her whole life would have changed for the better, regardless of whether her husband changed or not.

Something else would have been added to her life that would thenceforth brighten her days and smooth the bumps in the road.

34

Maybe her husband would be there for her and maybe he wouldn't. Either way, she would have begun to live graciously and with joy, despite what her husband did or did not do.

And that, dear reader, is the purpose of this book. I hope to make the truth about the age old battle of the sexes so clear that you will see the reason for the fall and how to stop failing and falling. You will be able to stop hating your partner or yourself, and you will be able to calm down. You will be able to begin to let go of the baggage of unforgiveness and begin to live free.

Even just seeing clearly that all couples are in the same boat—that we are all Adam and Eve redux, with each family replaying the old scene from the Garden of Eden—you will be able to be more forgiving toward your partner when you see that s/he too is lost and misguided. Having compassion (instead of resentment) your heart will soften. And when it does, the love of the Creator will flood your being.

- 5 -

More About Avoiding the Blame Game and Solving Your Problems

I am not going to play the blame game when it comes to public schools, government, or the clergy.

Instead I wish to focus on the two people involved— the two partners. Each of them and both of them can change their attitude and change the outcome for the better in a short time, perhaps days.

How is it possible, you ask, that a husband or wife can change their life and perhaps their relationship for the better within a short amount of time when the clergy, the counselors, the social workers, and thousands of experts and writers are failing to solve our individual and collective problems? When all these helpers and experts seem unable to solve the family violence that is everywhere, and the increasing statistics of broken homes, sexually transmitted diseases, and divorce?

After three thousand years of recorded history, humankind has not been able to solve cruelty, emotional abuse, heartaches, suffering, pain, and hurt feelings. The biggest victims of all are still the kids.

The reason why an individual person can do what all the experts and helpers can't seem to make happen is because the individual can change his or her attitude and acquire a new attitude of forgiveness, patience, and understanding. These wonderful attributes— forgiveness, patience and understanding—come from within. They come from believing instead of doubting what you know in your heart, and they come from accepting instead of resenting the gentle chastisement of conscience.

A person can literally have a change of heart, start meditating, and within a few weeks you won't even recognize them as being the same depressed, resentful angry person they were before.

We are always looking for someone else to do something for us, when the answer is within. A Heavenly order is waiting to unfold for the sincere seeker of truth and for the person who is willing to be more forgiving.

I will address this issue in greater detail elsewhere in this book. But right now I want to give you a sneak preview. The main problem that we all have—almost without exception—is resentment. Admit it, you resent your husband.

And you husbands—admit it, you resent your wives.

The first key to emotional well being and toward building a better relationship is to simply see and admit that you are resentful. And also judgmental. In fact, (and ladies don't get mad at me for saying this, but I've been counseling now for over 20 years)—women, in particular, have a problem with judgment.

What resentment and judgment do is block love. You cannot resent and love at the same time. You cannot judge another and have patience with them at the same time. Love comes from within. It is the love from our Creator that we all need. It is the healing balm and the ultimate fix.

But if you do not forgive others, then your Heavenly Father will not forgive you. He will not give you His approval and warm love if you are secretly resenting and judging your husband, for example.

Judgment is a very sneaky thing. A lot of women say "I don't resent anyone, and I'm not angry at anyone."

Yet they are secretly judgmental. Judgment is a "superior" sort of hate. Men, being the weak whimpering dogs or violent brutes that they are, are very easy to feel superior to. A woman can feel very superior to her man, judge him for his failings, and feel rather saintly or even martyr like (doing all she does for her ungrateful brute), and never suspect that she is actually hateful.

This judgment, which can become an addiction, separates her from love and is the a hidden cause of feelings of emptiness, low self esteem, unhappiness, and a host of related physical symptoms.

Again, I wish to emphasize that everyone knows when they are angry, most know when they are resentful, but quite a few people are very judgmental and never suspect anything wrong with it or see how it is subtly ruining their life.

And you husbands, how can you love your wife if you are resenting her?

So, whether you are a man or a woman, if you are sincere in your desire to know the truth, then reading this book will help you to forgive. Why?

First, it will open your eyes to see that you are indeed more angry, resentful and judgmental than you realized.

Secondly, you will start to see something wrong with these emotions. And third, you will see how we are all victims of the legacy of misunderstanding—and seeing this will make it easier to be more forgiving.

Your eyes will be opened about the nature of men and women, the legacy of failing that we all share, and the subtle evil which has penetrated the human race.

You will see that most people are victims of this process. Then the error of pride and its promoter, evil, prevents us from loving each other. It comes between the husband and wife and between the parent and child.

And how does it get inside of us? Mostly when we resented and hated our parents. Then when we grow up and become parents, there it is compelling us to be cruel to our children, to be willful, to resent our husband, and to use our wife.

It is always there operating through the no man's land of the subconscious and the imagination—feeding your ego with ambitious schemes and dreams, justifying your judgments, excusing your errors, helping you feel sorry for yourself, filling your mind with notions of grandeur, thoughts of revenge, and fantasies of sex and violence.

It is always there misguiding you and leading you into folly.

You followed it because you assumed that the thoughts that rise in a moment of temptation are your very own thoughts. But they are not.

And it is always there in our leaders and demagogues, teaching them to promise us glory and restored dignity, but leading us to individual and collective destruction.

There is no hope for you unless you wake up to see what is going on and stop following the voice that urges you, for example, to divorce your spouse and find excitement and pleasure in party time with someone else.

As your eyes are opened to what we are all up against, your heart will be softened. You will see that your poor old mom and dad were not being deliberately cruel.

They could not help themselves. No one loved them either. No one cared enough to show them the way.

You will see that your husband is just a man. You will see that he has not yet found the bond with his Creator within. You will see that he too is a victim and is lost; and you will no longer need hate him This does not mean you have to like what he does (if he is erring) or feel sorry for him, but you can see the failing without resenting him.

Husbands, you will see that when your wife was a girl, her father was undoubtedly not there for her. She went out into the world looking for love, and most likely all she got was use and abuse instead. You will see that the more she might tease you, tempting you to resent her, and the more confusing she is—that is your opportunity to shine. You can be all the more patient and longsuffering, all the more calm, and all the more reasonable.

Seeing that it is your role to be the Moses of the family, you will learn to become more fatherly. And as you grow in wisdom and patience, she will begin to respect you.

You will also see that most people are lost. You will see that most people do not have love. So you will stop craving guidance and love from them. You will begin to be patient with them, and as you are patient with others, your Heavenly Father will be patient with you.

Thus it will come to pass that you will be able to be patient with yourself too.

And being patient with your partner, you may become very good friends and live happily ever after.

Perhaps now you can see why I do not focus on errors the church, schools, universities, and government may be making. I cannot save the world, and for the most part, they are not interested in my help anyway.

They believe they already have the answers. They believe in evolution—that we are getting better, and that through technology, medicine, pharmacology, social sciences, and psychology we can solve all our problems.

They do not see that we are a fallen race. And that the more we meddle and try to solve our problems with technology and psychology, the more problems we create.

But I can help an individual--someone who is sincerely searching for answers and who really and truly wants to be a better mom, dad, husband or wife.

The other reason I do not focus on the societal level and point the finger at our institutions is because, in a way, they are doing the best they can.

When our love fails and violence erupts in the family, someone has to step in and restore order.

When men fail to be men and when they fail to assume their proper role as head of household, someone has to step in. Mostly it is mom who is left to handle things and raise the kids.

When dad is gone, a drunk, a drug addict, or off with some other woman, then mom has to do the best she can. Without a husband, she has to look to government to help her.

When a doctor, a lawyer, a counselor, a bureaucrat, or an educator is called upon to help someone, it is hard or even impossible to turn that person away.

Some of you know where I am going. The problem is not the government, the schools, or any other institution—if men would be men, the family would be much happier, and most problems would be nipped in the bud before they even start. But when father has left, when the husband is weak and unaware, when the man is selfish, and when he uses his wife instead of loving her—things are bound to go wrong.

Throughout this book you will see two important themes repeated over and over again.

1. The man must learn to be unselfish. He must learn to become more fatherly. He must find an invisible bond within, so that he can find the patience, the kindness, the longsuffering, the forbearance, and the wisdom he will need but does not now have. The man must learn to be a man.

2. The woman must stop resenting her husband and judging him. Since all men have failed her, her husband is undoubtedly failing her in some way. Her father was probably not there for her and now her husband is not either.

Having known nothing but failing men, the fallen woman cannot help but judge and resent him for his real or imagined failings. Then feeling guilty for her resentment and judgment, she misinterprets her guilt as being for not doing enough for him.

So she serves out of hate and guilt, and when she serves him, he just gets worse and takes more advantage—leading to another round of resentment and judgment. This is the treadmill of suffering on which all sinners are trapped until their suffering makes some of them wake up to see what they are doing wrong.

The woman, who begins to wake up and repent of her resentments and judgments, will be able to quickly climb out of the black hole of depression and the feeling that she always has to do more and more for others.

If there is any goodness in her husband, she must learn to appreciate what is good in a man. And if he fails, she must learn to see the failing but resist the temptation to resent him. If she does not resent or judge him, then she need not feel guilty for discerning his wrong. And if she is not guilty, she can forbear serving him out of guilt.

Less resentful, she can then be less willful, trying to change her husband or becoming impatient and bossy with the kids. By not resenting, she will find love within. And by no longer resenting him and meddling, she will give him the space to find himself. There may be a man in there, but right now her resentment of him makes it difficult for him to find himself.

In other words, both husband and wife have some basic training to do. This book is a good starting point.

The reason I do not spend more time in this book critiquing the failing of our social and governmental institutions to solve our problems is because they have been forced to take upon themselves something which is really something husbands and fathers should be doing.

Because of the weakness of men and their abdication of their responsibility, other people have had to try to fill the vacuum.

You see, it is the father who should be teaching morality and principles related to courtship, marriage and family.

The good example and the abiding concern and awareness of the good father are themselves powerful protectors and teachers of values, often without anything even having to be said.

The raised consciousness of the aware father tends to raise the awareness of everyone in his family.

They see, in the light of his raised awareness, what is right and reasonable, and they also see what to avoid.

Besides, the fact that the father is there for the kids, that he is involved, that he is emotionally available, and that his words and deeds make what is proper crystal clear are often all that is needed.

But when dad is not there for the kids or when he is weak or himself confused about values, then there is a vacuum that someone else must fill.

The job is transferred to mom, and she then transfers various teaching and value bearing responsibilities to daycare and school--to teachers, counselors, youth ministers, coaches, and various other people--many of who are really strangers.

Through the failing of fathers, it comes to pass that teachers, coaches, ministers, counselors, experts, and bureaucrats are charged with conferring values.

Somebody has to do it. And if nobody does it, then values of the peer group and the pop culture become the ones that are predominant.

My point is—when fathers fail, others have to do his job. Some do the best they can. Others take advantage of the vacuum and use it to promulgate some personal agenda that they have. But the fault is the default of father.

- 6 -

What the Clergy Gets Right and What They Don't

The clergy does a decent job of at least talking about pre marriage issues like abstinence, moral purity, avoiding promiscuity, waiting until you get married, and taking lots of time to find out what the other person's values really are.

But where the clergy is woefully weak, inadequate, and frankly sometimes misinformed is what to do about relationship issues within marriage.

Mostly they give you a hodge podge of Scripture verses mixed with a preponderance of psychological jargon. You get secular psycho babble with a few Scriptures thrown in.

They don't give you spiritual clues to dealing with mood issues. They don't give you fatherly wisdom about dealing with your wife, your husband, or your kids. They don't explain the negative role of parental and school pressure in contributing to kids' rebellion or drug use.

They don't teach how resentment and judgment are involved in depression or bipolar disorder. And they don't explain how resentment and impatience set us up to become over-reactive to stress, which leads to stress based PTSD and other ailments.

Instead, pastors, youth pastors, marriage pastors and Christian counselors often become pressure sources themselves. All too often they talk of Biblical principles which they really do not deeply understand themselves. They teach them and apply them in a mechanical way, but something is missing.

They talk about being nicer to our family in terms of compromise or being supportive, when being nice in a weak supportive way is often itself the cause of family problems. They talk about character—but frame it in terms of building someone's character, which is guaranteed to create a characterless conformist or angry rebel.

Where is the real wisdom and the delicate understanding? Where is the subtlety?

You will only find the wisdom and subtlety to gracefully deal with your spouse and kids if you, yourself, have the common sense and insight to apply what you had learned with understanding.

Any teaching, even a technically sound one or a Biblical one, if applied without understanding does more harm than good.

We are taught to look in the wrong place for wisdom. We are told to look to a book or some outside "expert."

Even the Bible itself tells us that "the letter killeth but the Spirit giveth life." The Bible is not the Word of God. It is a word *from* God. The words in the Bible should awaken us to realize the wordless Word within.

Christ said to the scribes and Pharisees "You search the Scriptures, but all they do is testify of *me*." The Bible testifies to the Wordless Word within. When what we read awakens us to the Inner Testimony, then the reading has done its job. The real living wisdom from God then takes over.

But when we are made to fixate on the external words of a preacher or a book, then the book becomes our god, and we miss the real life and understanding that come from God within.

"Behold the day is coming when and I will write my laws into their hearts. And I shall be their God and they shall be my people." The Bible testifies to the Spirit, even as the Spirit within bears witness to these words which are meant to awaken you and lead you back from your involvement with external people and words to an intimate relationship with your Creator within

What we really need is someone who can help us relate back to the wordless Word within which we perceive by our intuition. We need tutoring about how to become still and find the inner Light from God.

Relating to intuition (conscience) we move closer to God and begin to experience repentance for errors we have been making. Mostly we were unaware that we were even making errors. Or if we knew we were erring, we didn't know how to stop.

We failed and then fell into the thought stream where we rationalized and excused our behaviors. We tried to figure things out, worry and scheme our way out of trouble. When we failed, we looked to outside people (also failures) to run (and ruin) our lives.

But if we could relate to our God given intuition, we would begin to have understanding. When we have understanding, then we have just-in-time guidance to deal with each moment with wisdom and grace.

No one—neither our parents, our educators, our counselors, nor our clergy—are of much help in this regard. They should be, but they are not. Anything they have to tell us usually involves more study, more dogmas, more theories, more techniques, or more chemicals. They tell us just about anything other than what would really do us some good: how to relate to our God given intuition.

Anything but how to find the link to God and how to relate to the wordless advice God is trying to give us through our conscience.

How do you think the ancient prophets and the patriarchs got so wise? They didn't go to college or read books. And I know I will be accused of heresy, but they did not read the scriptures either.

They didn't ask experts, study or attend seminars. Many of them did not even go to church! They looked within and found a one on one relationship with their Creator. They worshipped God on their knees. And if they made an altar, it was one of rough stone so that God was glorified, not man.

They realized truth intuitively. They had vision because they saw things in the Light of Truth within.

They loved truth and they loved and yearned for God, and He responded by revealing Himself to them.

They did everything with love and wisdom. They walked with God.

Sure, they may have read something, but they read it with understanding. They had a real relationship with their Creator. Scripture only confirmed what they already knew.

They trusted God and looked to Him first. They did not look to raw knowledge to save them like we do today.

If you could become friends with your conscience, you would be brought to repentance and you would begin to realize the reason for your issues. You would quickly calm down, begin to have self control. You would find patience with yourself and with others. You would be re-humanized through God's help. And His help would come by way of the inner Light.

But as long as you fixate on study, look to experts on the outside or look into your rabid intellect (which is fed by outside suggestions and pressures) for guidance, you will fend off the inner Light.

Find intuition from God and your problems will soon be on the mend. It's that simple.

The special Christian meditation to learn how to be still is what you need.

Solomon was granted one wish. He could have asked for knowledge or wealth. But he asked for wisdom so that he could lead his people properly. This was the right thing to wish for because it leads to every other good thing. Find the inner Light, the source of guidance from your Creator, and you have it all.

But who teaches us this?

It should be your father who teaches you these things. Or the clergy. But they have not found the way to relate to God within themselves either. Their study has gotten in the way.

Besides, if you found your Creator within, all your problems would be solved and you would not need them. So they, and all the other experts and helpers, have a vested (though usually unconscious) interest in keeping you in the dark. They grow rich and powerful on your problems.

Learn to live intuitively and you will begin to calm down and you will begin to understand yourself and your partner.

If you are sincere in your search for truth—if you really and truly want to be a better wife or husband, a better parent, and if you are willing to admit that you don't know how to be one now--the simple technique of becoming still and getting out of thinking, together with some simple instructions about letting go of resentment, will get you on the road to recovery, and will get you started toward understanding others.

But don't expect much help from the shrinks, the clergy, the so called experts, or the educators in finding the inner way to God and understanding. They haven't found it themselves. They are very knowledgeable (too knowledgeable) and it gets in the way of seeing simple truths.

But never doubt that you have the capacity to discover truth within, solve your problems and learn to live a meaningful problem free existence.

Another thing I would like to humbly point out with love is that a large percentage of the clergy lacks the courage of conviction. Many of them have succumbed to the theories and values of Godless psychotherapy.

Many of the clergy and Christian counselors have bought into fashionable labels with questionable science behind them, such that of ADHD and bipolar disorder. Many ministers, counselors and church leaders have bought into the current fad of stating that mental health issues are due to "a chemical imbalance in the brain."

Nevertheless, I am pleased to say that a small but growing number of enlightened psychiatrists and concerned physicians, such as Dr. Peter Breggin, are countering the theory of a chemical imbalance in the brain. They are also questioning the power that the pharmaceutical industry has over mental health practices.

Timid and intimidated, many members of the clergy merely echo what DSM diagnosis someone had labeled the parishioner with. After the diagnosis and weeks, months or years of taking psychiatric meds, the minister or church counselors have nothing to offer the victim but some nice platitudes, verses to read, and some material to study.

The religious verses are little more than a form of positive thinking, where a person keeps repeating some affirmation hoping that the repetition and emotional investment will make it so.

Maybe the psychiatrist's meds, the minister's words and the church music will have a temporary placebo effect. But when the false reassurance wears off and real moral dilemmas and the spiritual issues that one senses deep in one's being are still found to be there—where will the person turn?

Why not teach the person how to find God within. But who can do so?

It's bad enough that the church has capitulated to secular psychology. But imagine the betrayal that must be felt when a person goes to a pastor with some questions about life and what it all means, and he is told that instead of thoughtfully pondering the meaning and purpose of life and searching for answers, he needs meds to balance the chemicals in his brain?

Instead of being related to as a human being with a soul, he has, in essence, been treated like an animal with chemical issues. Talk about being degraded!

It says in the Bible that in the last days the church would have the form of Christianity but would lack the power thereof. Many of our church leaders are powerless. They do not have love; they do not have the Spirit of God. They are weak and ineffective. Their only power is to deceive and bamboozle people with words, degrees, and clever events complete with slideshows and music.

Where are the David's, the Jeremiah's, the Daniel's, the Peter's, and the Paul's?

Of course, ministers and Christian counselors do quite properly talk about such things as forgiveness and patience, but they don't really know how to help people actually implement forgiveness or how to be patient.

Tainted with the secular, they appear weak; and in today's anti-Christian environment, they are not credible.

So I will say it again. The church has many good things to say about pre nuptial matters, such as dating, courtship and moral purity. But they are weak when it comes to the emotional issues people deal with in real life, and the church is weak when it comes to helping people who start to have emotional or relationship issues once married.

Most ministers usually do say the right things (as many of our parents do too) about pre marriage and courtship. What they say is often quite helpful. The principles are quite clear and not at all subtle. For example, the principle of avoiding sexual promiscuity and remaining sexually pure is absolutely true. Waiting until you are married is also true.

The Christian pastors and teachers also have many good and useful things to say about courtship. They warn about casual dating. They provide excellent advice about getting to know the other person. There are some excellent pre marriage seminars and books about Christian courtship. This is all good—it is Biblically sound, morally sound, and it is good common sense.

The trouble is that most of us don't follow their advice. We throw caution to the wind, and go with our feelings.

Another reason why we don't heed them is because the whole culture is pulling the other way. The movies, the songs, the public schools, and the so called experts are all saying things that contradict what we hear in church.

The pop culture, in particular, begins indoctrinating kids from age 10 or even younger with subtle and not so subtle sexual messages and promotion of a promiscuous lifestyle. Moreover, television and the movies are full of put downs of parents--portraying them as dumb, behind the times, or irrelevant. Ministers are portrayed as mean, rigid or as buffoons.

Casual dating is usually shown as something that kids just have to do.

If all this weren't bad enough, a shocking number of teachers, educators, counselors, and social workers believe that there is no use teaching abstinence because "they are going to do it anyway." (Which is not true).

This philosophy of causal dating, hooking up, doing your own thing and disregarding traditional values permeates the culture, the streets, the airwaves, the internet and the classrooms.

But nowhere is it more focused than on the youth. It is as if there were an unspoken desire that the morals of our youth should be broken down.

One wonders why principles governing the delicate spiritual union of two people would be suppressed or deliberately hidden. One wonders why--until you consider that there is a lot of money to be made in problem solving. The pundits, the counselors, the psychiatrists, the pharmaceutical companies, the divorce lawyers, the social workers, and the machinery of the law all make a good living off the ignorance, mistakes and suffering of people.

If everyone knew the principles and lived moral and principled lives, they would be happy, healthy, trouble free and successful. The problem solvers would all be out of business.

That is why so many so called helpers do not really, deep down, want you to get better. If you did, you would not need them anymore. If they gave you the true keys to successes, they would soon be out of business.

Besides, many of them are woefully ignorant and misguided. They do not know how to make their own lives happy, let alone anyone else's.

Many college teachers, for example, are attracted to social experimentation. They see it as modern and progressive, and they are quick to want to overthrow traditional values, which they see as an impediment to their lifestyles.

When asked why so many scientists were willing to embrace the theory of evolution, one of the founders of the movement said, in a candid moment, that "the idea of God interferes with our sexual proclivities."

Now let's return to the topic of marriage relationships. The proof of our folly and lack of understanding is everywhere. Arguing, fighting, hurt feelings, broken hearts, divorce, violence, financial ruin, and broken homes are just some of the consequences.

I can't argue with those of you who say that too many marriages are marriages in name only. A piece of paper will not make good an otherwise unhappy relationship. Of course, the converse is also true--just living together will not preclude the troubles that beset married couples.

It's not about the marriage license. It's about discovering what it is about men and women that leads to trouble, and it's about learning to be unselfish and being more forgiving. It's about a humble attitude of sincere inquiry and a willingness to admit your own part in what has gone wrong instead of blaming the other person. But my just telling you these things is not going to do you much good without a willingness to change.

It is well known among counselors that a drug addict or alcoholic will only make a complete recovery when he sees and admits he has a problem and when he really wants to change. Likewise, in a rocky marriage, a person has to admit that s/he has been selfish—he is his way, and she in her way—and admit that s/he is contributing to the problem before any meaningful change can take place.

Now that we have dealt with a few preliminaries, we are ready to look into what love is, mostly by showing you what love is *not*. Perhaps the best way for me to begin is by pointing out some of the popular misconceptions about marriage.

May this book open your eyes and help you to set aside the lies, falsities and misconceptions that surround relationships. It is also my hope that you will also be awakened to see and appreciate the mysteries of love that spring in your heart and bless your relationship. So fasten your seatbelt. Here goes.

- 7 -

Why Couples Argue

My relationships blog gets a lot of visitors. In a relatively short period of time, well over 10,000 people have arrived from Google search. By far the most Googled search terms that bring them to my blog have to do with arguing and fighting in marriage.

This does not come as any surprise to me. I know that couples argue. If it is any consolation to you, basically all couples argue.

You could almost say that all the squabbling and arguing are "normal." I would venture to say that if a couple isn't arguing--something is wrong.

If there is silence, then it is usually an eerie silence with buried resentment and hostility underneath.

Perhaps one person has completely capitulated and has become a repressed doormat.

Arguing is part and parcel of relationships. Men and women are different and live in different worlds. It is thus not surprising that there are disagreements.

Someone once said that a good marriage is a good fight. Yes, there will be arguments. But there is such a thing as a good fight.

A good fight is about *what is right*, not *who* is right. A good argument is when—instead of sniping, anger, violence, or a game of one upmanship--reason prevails.

It's like a spirited debate. If one point of view has more merit to it and makes better sense—then it is healthy when there is a debate and reason prevails. It is even better yet, if the one who held another view comes around to see the wisdom of the more reasonable one.

When *what is right* wins, then both partners win.

It doesn't matter who is right—husband or wife— principle and reason are more important.

If the wife is right about something, and the husband is mistaken, then she should prevail. However, it would be nice if husband and dad were graced with wisdom. It makes it so much easier for the family. Everyone likes to be able to respect father and dad. That is why he must have no vices and he should know what is right.

He should also have the courage of conviction to stand for what is right even if it makes him unpopular.

Needless to say, he should also have patience and kindness, and not be angry or violent.

The man is supposed to be the Moses, of the family.

A man graced with patience, kindness, wisdom, courage, honor and reason is respected by his family.

With superb skill and the power of reason underpinned with love and faith, he leads them safely through the many dangers and temptations that the world has to offer.

Instead of having to look to peers (who are often confused themselves) or to strangers, how nice it is for mom and the kids to be able to come to father for wise guidance and counsel.

When the man is weak, he abdicates his role. The woman is in charge by default. Some women like the power that comes from a man abdicating his manly role. But other women don't feel comfortable with the power and the responsibility he has heaped on her shoulders.

In many homes, it is obvious that she is the center of everything and dad has become a nonfactor or a weak yes man, backing up whatever she says.

She takes change of everything and often proceeds to spoil or nag the kids.

Like it or not, her authority is not the same as the man's. Soon some of the kids are in rebellion against her pressures and manipulations.

Dad may see what is going on, but if he speaks up at all it is usually in an angry resentful way. He may try to get his power back through violence, but this is wrong and graceless. He looks bad, and she looks all the better in comparison. The kids rally to mom, who is like a saint in comparison to her brutish husband. The whole family will soon be in revolt, and divorce is the likely consequence.

Most decent dads go to the other extreme, which is also error. They become too nice. "Nice" generally equates to weak. And weakness is wickedness. The dad who capitulates to wife and the experts who tell him to be nice thinks he has to be nicer: never offending, always worshipful and deferential. He thinks he has to make her happy, so he tries to do more dishes, talk more, or get some Viagra.

He is doomed to fail, because his weakness tempts others to walk all over him or have contempt for him.

His wife and kids need him to be the Moses or David of the family, knowing what is right, and having manly strength. Not anger or rigidity, but the courage of conviction.

Goodness without force is impotent. Just as a good policeman knows how to use force to restrain an out of control person from hurting himself, so a husband and dad has to stand for what is right. Firmly and sometimes sternly, dad has to stand for what is fair and sensible.

If he has a twinkle in his eye and love in his heart, he will always know the right measure, even if he has to be firm at times.

There is a big difference, for example, between an angry touch and calm restraining force. It is mistake to try to be everyone's friend. Your family already has plenty of friends; what you wife needs is a principled husband who stands for what is right and fair; and what your kids need is a wise dad who knows how to set limits and who knows how to say "no" to ego excesses and unreasonableness.

Many men throw in the towel and sit on the catbird seat letting her lead the family to rack and ruin.

In other families, the dad appears to be in charge, but she lets him be in charge—which is the same as her being in charge.

As I said, in most homes dad is decent but weak. His wife is in charge. She may do a good job, perhaps an excellent job. But dad's weakness tempts everyone to have contempt for him and probably resent him. And that is not good for them.

Remember weakness, just as much as violence, tempts others to resent. The kids sense that the proper order in the house is reversed. They are subject to mom's willfulness and the pressures of others—and the kids sense that it is because dad is weak.

Since the wife resents him for his weakness and the kids resent him for his abdication, soon rebellion and contempt are the inevitable results. The man is surprised when kids and wife throw him out and ask for divorce.

The problem, you see, is that he has made her into his god, the ground of his being. He married her to support his ego. But whoever or whatever supports your ego--

59

whether it be a wife, a drug or your work--will become the fix you need to sustain you.

That is how she gained the upper hand, and now that she is his center, she had the power whether she likes it or not.

The proper order of authority for the family is God at the head, then Jesus, then the father/husband, then the wife, and the kids.

When the center of a man's life is the Creator, he has a deep inner bond of faith. The goodness in him does not come from him so much as it comes through him.

He serves God for God's approval. And doing what is right and just, he stands in contrast to the rebellious and naughty world. He stands for something. His family respects him and may love him if they, too, come to share his love for what is right.

But when the man is selfish, he looks not to do what is right and just. He looks to satisfy his selfish ego.

Needing support for his ambitious rebellious lifestyle, he finds a slinky woman who agrees with him.

By defecting from God, he needs a center of being. No ego can stand alone. Now he has to lean on his wife, looking to her for validation and assurance.

Of course, she is at first glad to fulfill this role. The power gives her a sense of security, as she gets a man she can control. But as time goes by, it leads to profound insecurity. Sensing his weakness, she feels responsible for him. And deep down, she knows that he is weak and thus cannot be trusted one hundred percent. She enjoys the power but also resents having responsibility thrust upon her.

She feels responsible for everything that goes wrong. She is under a compulsion to serve him and the kids and try to make things right. She may eventually feel like she has to hold the whole thing together. Under the weight of this stress and worry, her health might suffer or she sees herself growing old.

Feeling responsible for everything, she starts to nag and motivate others to perform. The likely result is rebellion or they become lazy because they know that she will do things for them. This leads to another round of frustration for her.

In order to break free from the described cycle of frustration and compulsion, she just has to see what is going on.

It's her husband's fault, but she contributed to the problem through eagerly taking the mantle of authority and seeking to run everyone's lives. She will have to cease from seeking to rescue her spoiled or rebellious kids.

Now she will have to see the harm she has done and butt out of their lives. Secondly she will have to stop resenting her weak husband. Yes, he is wrong. But now she must see that she cannot make him into a man. In order to preserve her own soul, she must observe his wrong without resenting him. She must also decease from trying to change him.

Perhaps before marriage she sensed that he was weak, and she got a glimpse of what was coming.

Perhaps she did not want to play the role of temptress because she saw what it did to him and to her. But because of the way men are, about the only way she could catch a man is through playing the temptation game.

So she went along with the arrangement, hoping that he would become the knight in shining armor she had been waiting for. But when he falls for her temptation, he becomes a dog looking for his ego fix. And soon she will have utter contempt for him.

She is horrified to discover that the more she loves him, the more of a dog he becomes. The more she is nice to him, the more of a childish spoiled ego he becomes. And if she tries nagging him, he become rebellious and irresponsible, or else she has to keep motivating him to perform.

So they marry and soon there are kids. But what is wrong is that because she is in charge of his ego, she can turn him into a whimpering dog just by withdrawing her support. Furthermore, since she is in charge of his ego, she must now provide the motivation to ambition that all egos need to keep ambitiously pursuing their selfish goals.

If he is the ambitious type and successful in worldly affairs, then she is the power behind the throne, supporting and reassuring him when he comes home from a hard day of playing politics at the office, while bringing her his ill gotten gains.

If he is not particularly ambitious, then she sees it as her bounden duty to spur him on the achieve more. If he fails or if he begins to rebel from her pressure, then she has to nag him to get him to function.

If he fails outright, then she is obligated to comfort him. She will usually do so out of guilt, since she feels guilty for having pressured him. But she soon resents him and has to nag him just to get him to start functioning again.

The kids see this arrangement and they very quickly figure out who is really in charge. It is mom. They have to buckle under to her authority.

He is either overtly ambitious and achievement oriented or else he is more modest. If he is very ambitious, then he is likely to eventually transfer his loyalty to work or money. The power to motivate his ego is transferred from the woman to work or money.

She is then jealous of his new loves. He might very well discard his wife and find himself a "better" woman to match his upwardly mobile status. If they stay together, she resents him but takes advantage of the perks that go with his worldly success.

On the other hand, he might break down under the pressure: become sick, have a heart attack, or become impotent. She then has to comfort his ego in its failure.

If he rebels against her enslaving comfort, he might again turn to another woman or perhaps the bottle.

Of course many men soon sense that their authority has been compromised. Unfortunately, they try to get their authority back with violence. If they succeed, then she has to comfort and appease the violent beast. She hates him, but may revel in knowing that her appeasement and comfort only make him a bigger beast, and eventually he is destroyed.

Sensing that she is somehow responsible and in charge of the beast he is becoming, he may become full of rage over what he sees happening to himself. Hatred of a woman's (or mother's) domination lies behind a lot of violence against women. That is why many prostitutes are in danger—the men they service crave sexual support but then become full of rage when they realize they have been degraded.

For example, a man, who has been put down and made to feel inferior by his overbearing man-hating mother, develops a hatred of women because they remind him of his mother who he unconsciously hates. He might harbor thought of murder. He hates women for what they did to him, yet there is a female identity within him, the result of an identity exchange due to his hatred of his mother.

On the other hand, he might grow up to become a woman oriented man, who goes out into the world looking for a younger slinky version of his mother.

When he finds her, he makes her into his mother. In the process he becomes more of a woman himself.

Other boys who come from this type of home with a weak or violent father hate their weak or critical father and totally identify with the mother. Again, through identity exchange, the boy might begin to feel womanly and in order to try to feel more masculine go out into the world looking for women with whom he can feel masculine. Unfortunately, he is likely to take on even more female identity in the process because of the identity exchange in the temptation experience.

Sometimes the female identity takes over and he becomes a woman. He might look for men to interact with, hoping to take in some masculine essence. But the types he is with are themselves likely to have a female identity inside.

The daughter who hates her dominating mother will become like her mother. Chances are her mother is becoming masculine through interaction with her husband. And the daughter might just take in through transference this masculinity. The fact that she hates her father who is not there for her is only likely to transfer even more masculinity to her.

She might become a man herself, or she might go out looking to play the field, hoping to prove her femininity, only to take in more male.

All this confusion and secret distress has its origin in the weak father--the father who is selfish and uses women to support his ego. He is either overtly abusive or subtly so.

If he is not there for his daughter and does not become the noble knight for his wife, then his selfishness tempts them to hate him and hold him in contempt.

The intrigue, the craving for sexual ego support and the resulting identity exchange take place more subtly in marriage. Husband and wives come to resemble each other. And it is usually the man who becomes more and more woman inside. He gets her identity, while she takes his energy.

Thus it can come to pass that a married man can become a homosexual.

The woman suffers to see what is becoming of her husband and kids because of her ego supportive love.

But supporting egos is all she knows. She thinks she is loving them, but her love only makes them more demanding, rebellious or wimpy. They demand her support. Then they blame her. She tries harder to please, only to find them becoming more ungrateful and spoiled.

Some rebel against her love, and this can be the cause of drug addiction and alcohol abuse. Their ego, which she helped make more degenerate, then needs a lower form of support (drugs or alcohol) to help it feel right about itself.

But although she played a big part in their degeneration, it is not her fault. If the husband would be a real man and look to God for approval, he would stop demanding that the woman support his ego. There would be less sex, but it would be more fulfilling because it would be with love and not use. And if he was the noble father in the home, the kids would not become spoiled or go into rebellion against mom's supportiveness.

Father would be there with a gentle corrective love that would help them grow uncorrupted to be big but healthy egos. The kids would most likely grow to become self corrective. And if they love where their father is coming from, they will then be free to willingly choose that good Source too.

Most men are decent. They go to work and come home to watch television and read the newspaper every night. They can't understand what his wife needs, why she is never satisfied, or why the kids are acting out.

He can't understand why his kids are in rebellion or why his wife is unhappy. He doesn't see that his niceness is weakness. He doesn't see the harm that comes from making her into his god.

He doesn't realize that he thereby loses his manly authority. And no amount of violence can get it back.

The more angry and violent he is, the worse he looks.

It is only in reason, patience, longsuffering, courage, and honor that he can have the virtue to stand alone against the seductive temptations of the world.

When he turns his back on virtue and the Source of all good, the Creator, to be naughty or ambitious, and when he relies on the support of the woman, he is, without realizing it, giving himself over to the worldly order that has its roots in hell.

It is not the woman's' fault. When a man calls upon a woman to support his ambitious and selfish lifestyle, he draws upon a woman's dark side. He is really calling upon Satan, you see, to support him in his defection from God.

No wonder, the woman becomes bitchy and witchy.

It is the hell in her that becomes active because of the man's use of her.

What's a woman to do? Well, that's what this book is about. If you are already in a relationship, then stand back and see the dynamics as I have described them.

Begin by not resenting your husband. Your judgment and resentment only feed your contempt. And your contempt makes it harder for him to find himself.

By hating him you complicate things. Worse yet, you hurt your own soul through that hatred. This does not mean that you have to like what may be going on. Nor does it mean that you have to deny your feelings. Just don't add the pinch of resentment or the accompanying judgment.

If you are not yet in a marriage or long term relationship, then don't be flattered by the wooing of weak men. Look for a man of principle, one who makes what is right more important than anything. Watch out for the weak men who tip toe around and never offend you, because they want you to support them.

Likewise stay away from the womanizer, the drinker, the pot smoker, or the violent man. Life with them would be a living hell.

Men, if you recognize yourself in my description and you can see that you are selfishly using your wife--then knock it off! Don't make her into the ground of your being. Learn to do what is right and wise, whether or not she supports you in it or agrees with it.

A real man does not need support to do what is right.

Now you are ready to see why men and women fight.

Scenario one: She is in charge, through his abdication. She likes the power, being in charge and wants to be right all the time. His feeble or angry resistance only gives her more power until she becomes manly and sucks the life out of him.

Some women do not want the power, and marry a strong or violent man in order to keep herself in check.

But his anger or violence is wrong. As he responds to her angrily and as she cowers, all she does is help make him into a bigger beast. She is still in charge of his beastly ego development, you see.

The coward is in charge of making the bully a bigger bully. The bully, sensing that the coward is making him worse, takes out his wrath on the coward and becomes even worse.

Scenario two. She does not want to be in charge, but he is weak and places all the responsibility on her shoulders. She resents him. But because resentment is wrong, it makes her feel guilty. So in her pride, she thinks that what is going wrong is her fault. She tries even harder to make things work. He on the other hand capitulates or rebels. Either way, he is wrong, tempting her to resent him. Again she feels guilty and serves him out of guilt.

In some relationships, he keeps failing and being irresponsible, and out of guilt she keeps accepting him back. Soon he is back to his old ways, and the whole cycle repeats itself.

Both are selfish and wrong, and they are playing the usual game of ego one upmanship. He sees her wrong and resents her for it, and she sees his wrong and judges him for it. They are fixated on each others wrong, but trapped into a codependent relationship through resentment and guilt. Nothing good can come of this.

Usually one side is more awake and unselfish than the other. The one who is aware and wants to do what is right seeks to get the other to cooperate with what is fair and based in common sense. But the other person argues or undermines, tempting the one who was more right to become resentful or unreasonable. Thus the reasonable one gets pulled down to the level of the wrong one.

In this situation, if you are the one that is reasonable (just make absolutely sure that you are right), then continue to make your points with calmness. Do not get sucked into a no-win argument. State your points and, if you can, do what is right or wise. Do not resent the other person. Be unwilling to capitulate to wrong on the one hand, but don't get pulled into emotional arguments. If you find yourself getting sucked in, then stand back.

Scenario 3: The man is basically decent and is attempting to assert his head of household authority.

But she is naughty and willful and seeks to undermine or countermand his instructions. If she is very naughty or even wicked, she will even seek to undermine his authority with the kids, perhaps turning them against him when his back is turned. The temptation is for him to stop patiently expressing truth and holding the line, and instead become resentful, frustrated and throw in the towel.

In this case, he must continue to stand for what is right with patience and firmness, but without resentment. It is okay to make his points forcefully, as long as there is no resentment. Resist the temptation to be angry, to be violent, or to leave and go to the bar or another woman.

Resist the temptation to give in to her unreasonableness. Hold the line. Stay the course.

Don't flinch or run. State your points calmly. Suffer in quiet dignity. Do not look for support from anyone—be it a wife, friends, colleagues, clergy or support group. Look to your Creator within.

Scenario 4: She wants him to be the man of the family but he is like a big baby or weak and selfish. She resents him, and in her resentment becomes guilty.

Then she serves him out of guilt, only making him more selfish. She might be arguing to just try to make him aware that she wants him to do his share of the responsibility.

In this case, he should realize that he is wrong. He should see the harm that he is doing by being weak and using her. He should apologize, admitting his weakness, and tell her that from now on things will be different.

He should not become emotional or say "can you forgive me?" Only God forgives. Asking another to forgive you puts them in the role of God. Instead simply apologize, say you are sorry, and say "I have not been the man I should be, but from now on things will be different." Then go about your business and clean up your act.

The woman in this scenario is a decent woman and suffers greatly for his weakness. She would like him to do his share, but he won't. I cannot say whether she should wait patiently to see if he finds himself and realizes his wrong, or whether she should draw a line in the sand.

If it's a short term relationship, it might be best to take leave of him. If he is weak and irresponsible, there is probably no future with this man.

On the other hand if she suspects that there is some good in him, she might wait and see.

Each situation is different, so I cannot say what to do about staying or going.

But one thing I know for sure. She can watch for resentment and let it pass. Resist the temptation to resent him and judge him. Resist the temptation to serve him out of guilt (for resenting him). Resist the temptation to feel sorry for him (also based in guilt). Resist trying to change him. Stand back. Be objective.

Let resentment pass.

Quietly grow in grace. In fact, your graciousness will either shame him into repentance; or if there is no good in him, it will make him so uneasy and he may run off. If so, good riddance to bad rubbish.

Another form of arguing is when both people are basically resentful. He for his reasons, and she for hers.

Both clam up and shut down, but there is suppressed hostility which occasionally erupts into arguments. Or it results in being critical and negative due to the resentment. On the surface everything appears fine, but underneath there are resentment and hurt feelings, perhaps bitterness. All these suppressed feelings contribute to emotion based illnesses.

Most of us are so busy worrying about our own needs that we fail to see our own wrong. Many of us are selfish and do not see the other person's true needs.

Many of us are not right ourselves, so we are defensive and guilty. We get upset and irritated over little things that don't really matter; and we clam up and say nothing about important things that should be addressed.

We must learn how to argue the right way (where *what* is right wins, not *who* is right). And we must learn to make our points without resentment and anger.

And before I go any further, let me say that it is basically the man's fault. I personally think that women suffer more because they are more aware of something being wrong. Men tend to be kind of dumb in such matters. Men tend to think that just going to work and taking her out to dinner once in a while is all that is needed. He just doesn't get it. .

But it is ironic that it is the man who is supposed to be the dispenser of wisdom. The man is supposed to have understanding and wisdom, and from it longsuffering and patience. Instead many men are like big kids. So, men, please take careful note of what I have to say.

If he could learn to be more fatherly and stop demanding that she support his ego; then she could stop playing the role of tease or nag. If he had real love, she would not have to tease him for it (only to be disappointed again). And when she was finally assured that he loves principle more than anything in the world, so that he would never fail her, she could stop giving him such a hard time. All the bickering could stop, and they could become very, very good friends.

Ladies, now that I have placed responsibility for what is going wrong squarely on the shoulders of the man, let me say that your problem is most likely that you just can't resist judging him for his failings.

Yes, all men (including the author) have failed women, and so they are ooooh so judgeable. But I have to say that judgment is a terrible sin. It fixates you to the object of judgment, and by way of guilt (for the judgment) locks you into an endless cycle of love and hate. It leads to deterioration in your being and to bitterness.

When we become quite resentful and judgmental, we find it almost impossible to be objective. A resentful wife can become so hateful toward her husband that she literally cannot see any good in him. Even if he improved, she would not see it.

The ability to stand back and look at the situation objectively is of absolute importance. That way, error can be observed without resenting what one sees.

Another's wrong can be observed without judging (hating and condemning) the other for it.

So, if you are like most couples, you are arguing all the time. As long as there is no violence, then perhaps all you need is to read my book and listen to some of my radio programs.

Because men and women are different, because most couples bring baggage to the marriage, and because there is so little wisdom out there--many young couples don't have much of a chance (without a little coaching from someone with understanding).

Probably you have bought the cultural foolishness about what love and what marriage are all about. Love is not sex; nor is it just hearts and flowers. Nor is marriage just for pleasure or getting our needs met. If we buy into the popular misunderstandings about marriage, then we will feel cheated, deprived of getting our needs met, and we will be resentful.

Before I go any further, let me just say that sometimes one person is a very disturbed or terrible person. This is exceedingly difficult for the other. But in this chapter, I will address the more common situation, where both are basically decent--not perfect, of course--but decent.

There is always hope in such a relationship that a positive change may occur. .

Let me also say that when misunderstandings occur--and they will occur--both partners often become so fixated resentfully to the other's wrong that neither really looks at their own attitude. So for the moment, put aside picking apart the other's wrong. Stand back and see if you can look objectively at the relationship between men and women in the light of what I am about to say.

If received with a spirit of humble inquiry, it could be a life changing break-through for you. You will see that all couples around the world are in the same boat: they are struggling without understanding. And so, they begin to resent each other instead of understanding what is really going on.

A whole lot of soul searching, a change of heart and willingness to give up resentment, judgment and blame are part and parcel of maturing and learning not to be selfish. Then perhaps all you need is a little basic training about the nature of women, the nature of men, and a little understanding about our fallen human race.

You might be able to salvage your marriage, with the two of you becoming very good friends and perhaps living happily ever after.

My authority for this assertion is intuition, whereby we know without words in the inner light of conscience.

I'm just a little closer to my God-given intuition than some others are. I am also fortunate to be able to put into words what I see. Because I am so blessed, it is my responsibility to share it with others. That's all.

And since I am not involved in your (the reader's) particular situation, I can be more objective, because I have no vested interest.

Because the same light that is in me is in you: if you set aside judgment and resentment, you can see what I see.

As you see it, you will see why you must not be resentful. You will see why you must give up blame.

When your vision is not clouded by hurt feelings and blame, you will be able to see the solution. Instead of being fixated to the problem, you will be "fixated" to the solution.

The evidence that what I say about the man/woman relationship is true is all around us. You probably know couples among your friends and family--who you know for sure are good people—yet who are making terrible mistakes, fighting and hurting each other. You wonder why they can't just stop arguing and just love each other. It is only in the light of understanding that their error makes sense. You will be able to avoid the same mistakes and perhaps one day even help them.

Marriage is not just two animals coming together.

People have souls, and the human race has a history. And marriage has a purpose. It is an institution ordained by God to bring children into the world, and a framework within which to learn not to be selfish.

There is an ancient mystery between men and women going all the way back to the Garden of Eden. And there is a legacy of misunderstanding that is passed down from one generation to the next. It is hard to convey all I wish to say in just a few paragraphs, but I can provide a few hints to get you thinking along these lines.

Divorce is not the answer. Just living together is not the answer. Just lovey dovey flowers and candy is not the answer. What is needed is understanding.

All the arguing and bickering that people have observed in their parents has led some people to try to avoid marriage by not getting married (by just living together). The same dynamics that occur in marriage occur in living together. The only difference is that without the formality and honor that is found in holy matrimony, living together is more likely to degenerate and fall apart. Sometimes the truth is that one person is not fully committed in their heart to the union.

I am not saying that just going through the motions of a ritual will make a bad marriage good. All I am saying is that marriage is an institution, a framework ordained by God, in which to work out the ancient mystery between men and women. Just because there is one bad marriage does not mean that the institution of marriage should be rejected; no more than just because there is one bad mayor, that the office of the mayor should be abandoned.

Am I saying that people who are living together are condemned? Of course not! What is needed is not condemning or condoning. What is needed is understanding. But again, my basic point is that living together is not a way to avoid the squabbling we saw in our parent's marriage.

Abraham Lincoln once said that two people should be able to disagree without becoming disagreeable.

Arguing, especially if done in the right way, gets things out on the table and is better that the typical eerie silence with resentment and secret hostility underneath. If one person is unreasonable--it should just draw forth more reasonableness in the other.

Remember: what is right is more important than who is right. When right prevails, then it is a win-win for both.

For example, let's say that one partner in the relationship wakes up, sees their selfishness, sees their part in the problem, drops resentment, drops the blame game and is ready to be a better partner. Let's say the other partner continues to tease, taunt, misbehave, and continues to be unreasonable. This will be a test, perhaps a severe one, of the sincerity and commitment of the one who has gotten better.

If he (or she) should continue to shine, do his (or her) duty, and not become resentful or bitter--it inspires respect and a feeling of security in the kids.

Especially if it is dad. They see that dad's love is not overcome by mom's resentment or unreasonableness.

They marvel at his invisible means of support. And they respect his beyond, and may one day wish to find what he found: His love of and inner bond with His Creator.

Reason, patience, and fairness win. One day the other partner may wake up too, because of the true love of the other.

What is the answer? Understanding. Each of us must wake up and begin to see our own selfishness. We must honestly admit that we are often more interested in our own comfort and ego needs. And when things get a little stormy, we are more intent on proving we are right and winning than in than the well being of the other.

We use another's wrong to puff up our ego in judgment, and then we use their wrong as an excuse for our behavior.

For example, many a resentful wife will serve her husband out of resentment. Her service is a way of making up for the guilt of secret hatred and judgment.

Her service also makes her feel like a martyr, sacrificing herself for someone who doesn't appreciate her.

Can you see why this sort of service is based in hatred? Because it is not out of love (but out of guilt for the resentment). Everyone outside the family thinks she is wonderful. But things are not always what they appear. Those within the confines of the family sense something wrong. The sensitive ones see the hypocrisy and reject it. Those who are bamboozled buy into a lie and become converts to phony love.

Another type of wife or mother uses all her work and service to validate her goodness. What she does has a hidden agenda. Everyone in the family is required to see her in a certain light; and those that don't, receive the brunt of her wrath.

Men tend to use sex or work to validate their manhood. But much more is required to be a real man.

Remember, humans are a fallen race. We have fallen from what love is all about to become creatures who need lies and ego reinforcement to reassure us. We fell from an agape emotionless love to sex love. Humans originally were meant to live forever. But when Adam defected from God's way, instead of regenerating perpetually through God's light, love and approval received within; Adam fell to having to generate sexually. He came to know the life that leads to death, the animal way of making replacement bodies to carry on.

That is why sex represents failing. Of course, it serves a good purpose: bringing children into the world. But sex is not supposed to be used for ego reinforcement.

But that is exactly what most men use it for. It is a fix to reassure their wobbly ego that the animal is what a real man is all about.

Actually a real man is the one who eventually learns to moderate his sexual practices out of consideration for his wife. He is the one who makes what is right more important than who is right. He begins to live for principle. He becomes more fatherly.

I also must say that marriage is not meant to be a pleasure party. The main benefit of marriage is to bring children into the world. And a secondary benefit is that once in marriage, we can learn to be unselfish. Before marriage, we can avoid seeing many of our failings, but marriage will bring them to the fore. If we learn and mature, marriage can be a great school.

There is an old joke about marriage being like a three ring circus: First the engagement ring, then the wedding ring, then the suffering. It's a joke, but there is a lot of truth in it.

Most of us do not know how to suffer properly. The egotist suffers egotistically and resentfully. But for the sincere person, suffering awakens us to search for answers: to ask "what have I done to bring this on myself?" During the searching process, the sincere seeker learns to suffer in quiet dignity, not resentfully.

Suffering properly can actually be a good thing. It is sobering and chastening. It leads to humility and thoughtfulness. It engenders respect in others.

Most men get married for the wrong reasons. They find someone who supports their ego or makes them feel good. They later discover that this gives her the power. She becomes the god of his fallen animal ego.

She motivates him to be ambitious and when he begins to falter, she nags and teases him to get him functioning. He feels trapped with a woman boss.

She, on the other hand, was aware of his weaknesses before marriage; but she thought her love would turn him in the prince. If she is a decent woman, she hoped that he would be the knight in shining armor who would rescue her from her unhappiness. But when he turns out to be an oaf; and when her love, instead of making him better, makes him more of an oaf, she becomes resentful. She begins to nag him and make demands, trying to whip him into shape.

Often he does respond and perform, though some men rebel to another woman or the bottle. She nags him and motivates him to work, only to later discover that he becomes married to money or his work. She feels betrayed.

Some women are glad to take advantage of the situation, and he becomes the work horse. On the surface, everything appears to be okay, but it is a shallow existence and a materialistic one without true love.

In some families there is fighting. In others a resentful peace (with both partners being resentful, bitter and angry underneath).

So what is the answer? The answer is to begin to wake up and realize that humans are metaphysical beings. Men have a beyond and women have a beyond.

In the Garden of Eden, Adam's beyond was heavenly principle. But he turned his back on it. Eve's beyond was the dark side, with the serpent's clever beguiling behind it. When Adam turned his back on God through doubt and disobedience, he became subject to the woman and her beyond.

Bear in mind: it was not her fault. It was Adam's fault for using her to pursue his secret ambition.

That is why marriage must be the woman joining herself to the man, and if he is principled and decent, to his beyond. Not vice versa. She will be rescued from her dark world and brought into his brightness. But God help the man who reverses the order and joins himself to her and her dark side. All hell will break loose, and his life won't be worth a plugged nickel.

Sometimes the woman wakes up first, and stops the game playing. The contrast of her brightness and modesty will shame him into awakening. If he welcomes the truth, and is willing to change, then both will live happily ever after. If he is stubborn in his selfishness, he may run off to another woman or the bottle. If so, "good riddance to bad rubbish" as the old saying goes. There simply is no future with an incorrigible selfish egotist.

But at the present time, chances are both are so involved in resenting and judging, that they can't really know the heart of the other. Men, look at your own selfish use and be more considerate of her needs.

Ladies, watch your own judgments, and stop giving your husband such a hard time that he doesn't have the space to find himself.

We must also wake up to see that we have been resenting and blaming the other person. Most of us are basically selfish. We have an agenda we want to impose on the other. When our needs are not met, we become resentful and begin to look elsewhere.

Some people are troubled by their own selfishness.

They wish to understand what is going on and seek true answers. It is for these people that I write. Don't expect a lot of help from the world. Most of the so-called experts give more of the kind of advice that obviously isn't working. They may be well meaning, but their advice is ego supportive. What we really need is the Truth that awakens and corrects aberrant egos.

So, what if you are in a troubled marriage now? If you are the man, chances are you are angry. She is not happy with anything that you do. She is in charge of your life. You have seen that anger does not work.

Express it and you look bad, get in trouble, or become a tyrant. Repress it and you get tummy aches and headaches or worse; besides, everyone has contempt and walks all over you. Neither extreme is good.

Of course, anger management helps. But only as a quick fix to teach you some behavior modification skills or how to transmute your anger in work or sports instead of violence. But what you really need is understanding: you need to see and be sorry for your selfishness.

You will see that anger is born in selfishness. But you will also see that wimpiness is copping out from your role of dad and father. If anger gives her power, then wimping out and handing control over to her does the same. Many decent men become total wimps because they are afraid of what they might say or do when angry, so they clam up and say nothing.

The man must search for the wisdom of Solomon and the patience of Job. He must learn how to stand for what is right in a no-nonsense way, but without anger.

He must learn to be kind and considerate. He must learn to stand for principle. He must learn to be more fatherly.

Of course, a good aunt, grandma, or uncle's advice can be very helpful with your marriage woes. They have been there, and they have the wisdom of years. But for the most part, your journey of discovery will be a solitary one. You must learn to stand back and observe with objectivity. Seeing the big picture of a situation will permit you to see why you must not become angry, why you must not resent, and why you must seek in your heart for what to say or do.

If you do not know how to stand back to get the big picture, get the meditation we have at the Center for Common Sense Counseling. It will teach you how.

What is needed is understanding. You need to understand what is going on, so that you won't over-react. For example, gentlemen, if you begin to see your wife as a person instead of an object of use, your understanding will begin to mitigate your behavior. You will become more considerate, less angry, and more fatherly.

Ladies, perhaps your searching will lead you to see that what you are really looking for is the father you have never known. Most dads lack an inner bond with the Creator. Most men are women oriented instead of God centered. They do the best they can, perhaps being good providers; but without the inner bond with their Creator, they cannot give the love they do not have.

What we all need is agape, emotionless love--the kind of love that comes from God. This love is not a feeling.

It is corrective of our ego excesses. It leaves us feeling chastened and throws us back on ourselves. In the Light of Truth we see our error, and we become self corrective. True love has a humbling quality to it. And afterwards, we have a sense of joy and freedom. True love is liberating. Such love can be in another person (who gets their ego out of the way). But it is not from the person. It comes through them.

If we see it in another, especially our father, it is a wonderful thing. But ultimately, we must search within, and if we are blessed, find it within. Here is a hint: You may find it when you are willing to drop your judgments and resentments against others. When you forgive others, then your Heavenly Father forgives you, and when you no longer seek the ego supportive love of the world, you are rewarded with His warm love from within.

The truth with love is supposed to set us free. But few of us have the love to set others free.

I once had a listener who could not understand why she so resented her husband. He was decent, hard working, honorable, always there, and kind. But he lacked something special (a love that comes through him from God). I explained to her that she was looking for something from him that he could not give. She came to see that her husband cannot give what he does not have.

This was a profound insight for her. She realized that he had not found love from God. Thus he too was empty and suffering. When he had been a little boy, he was hurt and damaged; and he never fully recovered. He could not give what he had not found.

An insight like this, if realized deeply, can lead to being able, for the first time, to drop resentments against the other person. And when you forgive the other person, then your Heavenly Father forgives you.

Just beyond forgiving others and dropping our grudges and judgments, comes the healing fulfilling love from God to warm our soul.

Ladies, you cannot make a man into a man. Even if you were to succeed, he would be in your image with you as his god. You would never be happy with your re-creation.

Men, do not look for love from your wife. Give love instead. Become more fatherly. Look upon others as if they were naughty school kids. Set a good example. Be forthright, but kind. Do not have expectations as to what the other person should be like or do. Be there for your family.

- 8 -

Myths of Marriage

A country philosopher once said "it's not so much what you don't know that hurts you, it's what you know that ain't necessarily so."

Nowhere is this saying more apt than when it comes to relationships. So here are some of the things we "know" that ain't necessarily so.

Myth: "Sex is love."

Most people believe or don't question this lie. Belief in this lie is just about universal even though experience has shown it not to be true.

For example, we all have either been taken advantage of (in the name of love) or we've known people who have been taken advantage of. Somebody said "I love you" just to get what they wanted. Or someone conned someone into sex to "prove that you love me."

Others have hooked up, and as relationships have come and gone, it's just plain obvious that whatever is going on, it certainly is not love.

Yet the fallacy is still universally expounded and believed. I guess hope springs eternal. Perhaps unless we call it "love," we have to come face to face with what sex really represents in reality. Sex, you see, is the first outcropping of sin. It is the evidence of failing.

Our modesty and a natural sense of embarrassment about sex proves that the human race has a memory of an original shameful fall a long time ago at the beginning of our human race.

And you thought the Garden of Eden story was a myth!

I know that right now those who hate where I am coming from are already twisting my words and saying that I am condemning people, trying to put us back into the days of the Puritans, or trying to spoil all the fun.

Nothing could be further from the truth. That sex is not love does not mean that there isn't such a thing as sex with love.

You can do anything with love. You can speak with love, and you can cook with love. You can install a swing in your backyard for the kids with love. And you can have sex with love.

All I am saying is that sex does not *equal* love. I will go into this in more detail later. Right now I want to make sure that my words are not distorted. I am not condemning. I am saying that our sexuality needs to be understood, not condemned. That's all.

Now I will continue with my explanation, if you care to read on.

All you have to do is remember the most recent example among your friends of some lady who was told by some cad that he loved her, only to be used by him and then he ran off.

All the broken hearts that have resulted from believing this lie and then giving in and giving up your purity are a testimony to the fact that sex is not love.

Many of us who are now older and wiser have had enough or seen enough bad experiences to be disabused of any notion that sex is love. Yet the myth lives on.

Sex is sex. But there can be, and should be sex with love.

In a marriage, sex is for the purpose of having kids and building a family. And when there is love, then it is both a useful and also a wonderful thing. That's how children come into the world.

But there is also just plain sex. Let's consider two different varieties of just plain sex. Outside of marriage. And inside of marriage.

First outside of marriage. Frequently a lady goes along with the pressure and gives in because she is afraid that if she does not give in, then she will lose the guy to someone who will give in. So she gives in to keep the relationship.

Often the woman is afraid that if she does not surrender her virginity, the man will go elsewhere. This is unfortunate. If he really had love (or at least a sense of propriety and honor), he would not require this of her. He would not pressure her.

Some ladies will virtually throw themselves at a guy in order to do what she thinks she has to do to prove her love. Would you believe that the fallen female ego is so constituted that some women are offended if he would rather not go all the way. Similarly, many women are secretly offended if you do not like their food.

A lot of guys are decent. But there is some sort of pressure out there—from the media, on the street, in the locker room—that to be a real man you have to have "done it." And in some circles, the more ladies you have taken advantage of the more of a man you are said to be.

This is obviously untrue. But I'm sure you have heard of how strong peer pressure can be. In fact, you have probably experienced it yourself, and you have probably succumbed to it.

There is peer pressure to take drugs, pressure to drink, and pressure to smoke. There is peer pressure to dress a certain way, talk a certain way, and listen to certain music. There is peer pressure to join a gang.

And there is peer pressure to engage in premarital sex or to be promiscuous.

Parents quite properly worry about peer pressure, and rightly so.

I'm sure you have heard of kids joining a gang for self protection. I'm sure you have heard of kids smoking just to be cool and not be accused of being a nerd.

Same thing with sex. Some kids are fortunate to be close to their family and not involved with groups of pre adolescents or adolescents who pressure them.

Some kids are strong and have a good moral compass; so strong that they just don't pay attention to the pressure.

But most kids in America today are very group oriented. In fact, group activity, called socialization skills, is what is promoted in the schools. Parents want their kid to be popular. And when popularity trumps principle, then morality goes out the window.

Dad winks if his kid smokes. Mom takes her daughter for human papiloma virus shots, because, after all, "they are going to do it anyway."

No wonder that kids shrug their shoulders and go with the tide.

Myth: "They will do it anyway."

Now we come to another big lie, one that is disrespectful and degrading to teens and to human beings and their capacity for reason, goodness and altruism

The lie is this: "they will do it anyway." You know the old line about "they will do it anyway so we might as well give them condoms and contraception."

The truth is that plenty of teens and young adults around the world are NOT doing it anyway. Expectation is a powerful thing.

Why is it that native born kids are failing and can't do math or read, but kids come here from Sri Lanka and win spelling bees and science contests? Why is it that kids from Korea, India, and Taiwan come here and get straight A's in math and become engineers?

The reason is parental involvement and parental expectations. It is simply expected that the kids will study and do well. So they do.

Have you heard the story of Roger Bannister? Before him, it was said that no one would ever run a 4 minute mile. So no one did until Roger Bannister did. Then runners started running sub 4 minute miles routinely. People knew they could run a sub 4 minute mile. So they did.

Many kids and young people around the world know they can be chaste until marriage. So they are.

There are plenty of happy, sociable, smart, well adjusted teens and young people around the world who are chaste and pure until marriage. It is simply expected.

Somebody wrote a book called the *Myth of the Teenage Brain*. In it, the author shows how teens throughout history have done great things. He points out a whole long list of great historical people who did great things when they were young--including some of the founding fathers of our country. Look it up. They weren't all old with grey hair.

My point is that the vast majority of teens and young adults are decent, good, smart, and capable of discipline and dedication. They just need society, parents, and educators to back them up a little instead of abandoning them to promiscuity, disease, broken lives, and moral failure. If the media and the schools think so little of your kids, why do you, as a parent, think so little of your kids?

Today in America we have it all backwards as a society. Instead of having high expectations of our teens, instead of creating conditions where abstinence is expected and rewarded; where there is proper supervision on the way from school, after school at home, all around town, and in the dorms; and where kids and teens always have a proper and watchful parent, grandparent, or loving responsible relatives around--we do just the opposite.

Promiscuity is expected, and it is subtly and overtly winked at or even promoted in songs, movies, on television and in the pop culture. There is a woeful lack of supervision. A nice lady doctor wrote a book called *Unprotected* to describe what kids face when they go off to college, and she is right. Some colleges even have coed dorms. What do you expect will happen?

In a kind and loving society, the children are allowed to be children. And young people are expected and required to be chaste and pure. Of course there will be some hanky panky. But very little. And it will be of the innocent variety—like holding hands or sneaking a kiss.

In a kind and loving society, everyone is organized to protect the virginity and morals of the kids. But when premarital pregnancy does (rarely) occur, then the family and society are organized to rally round the young mom, support her and love the child.

If possible, the dad should be there to get married. If not possible, then mom has her baby, and she either keeps it or it is put up for adoption. The family rallies to her aid and will help her raise her child and support her in any way they can.

But today we get it backwards. Everything is designed to virtually assure promiscuity. Then when the inevitable happens, society is there to see to it that the unborn child is killed with a morning after pill (which causes abortifaction) or killed through abortion.

The ubiquitous talk about condoms and frequent giving them away like candy conveys a not so subtle underlying assumption: you are going to do it anyway.

A big thing is made about how the condoms are for preventing sexually transmitted diseases. Yet it is well known that condoms are, for various reasons, not entirely effective at preventing the spread of sexually transmitted diseases.

What is effective, in fact *100 percent effective* at preventing sexually transmitted diseases, is abstinence.

But in an upside down Alice in Wonderland society, abstinence is frowned on.

With society so ill informed and heartless, the pressure is everywhere to give up one's morals and give in to promiscuity because "they will do it anyway."

Some kids don't succumb. In fact many don't.

Despite their weak parents, despite the amoral school system, despite the media lies—they don't go along with the pressure.

Some kids are smart and wise; they find a decent crowd to hang with. Some kids just pretend they have "done it" just to get others off their backs.

Some kids are busy with studies, sports, and planning for a career. They just don't get into situations that are fraught with danger.

I hope you have gotten the point. If you buy into the "sex is love" lie, or if you shrug your shoulders and sheepishly go along with it—if you don't say with kindness, compassion, but with blunt honesty that sex may be a lot of things, but one thing it is not is love—there is a danger that you child will go along with the lie and thus lose their virginity because, after all, "sex is love." And everyone wants to be loved.

If you parents go along with the lie that "they will do it anyway," then who will uphold the truth for your child? Kids are, after all, just kids. What is a parent for, if not to make what is right unmistakably clear and then uphold it themselves?

A lot of what goes on in the dating scene is use and abuse.

Men tend to be more sex oriented than women. It is usually the man, though not necessarily so, who pressures for sex. But as I said, this is for his selfish gratification. It is definitely not love. If it is consensual and if it leads to a marriage or long term relationship, then it is at best a form of use. If he really were a man of principle and not selfish, and if he really respected her, he would not pressure her nor would he want to use her to gratify his lusts before marriage.

To him it may not feel like use at the time (though his conscience will bother him afterwards). But it feels like use to her. She senses deep down that he is taking advantage at some level. And no matter how many nice frills and fancy terms like 'love" she puts on it, there is a sense that she gave something of value up.

This use of the woman for sexual gratification is harmful to him too, in that as his beastly side is reinforced and rewarded, he loses his character.

When he is not required to make a commitment (in both word and deed) and prove his honor by waiting until marriage, it gets things off on the wrong foot.

Later on, she will resent him. Especially if she has been used or abused before. When she sees that he is just like some other man who used her, she will never again have the same respect for him.

Now let's discuss plain sex within the context of marriage. The nice thing about marriage is that it is a formal commitment. Therefore you can feel more secure that you are giving yourself sexually to another person who really has made a formal commitment.

Another good thing about marriage is that it isn't long before the idea of starting a family comes to mind. Kids are a joy and a blessing. They are the first fruits of holy matrimony.

All other things being equal, for the young married couple the consummation of the marriage is pleasurable and has its delights. That's the way God made it. He wouldn't have made it so much fun if He hadn't intended the couple to enjoy each other.

After the delights of the honeymoon and the youthful joys of the springtime of marriage have been enjoyed, chances are children have come along. Now it is time to be more responsible and sober minded and time to set aside some of the youthful delights of earlier days.

Often the husband is still more interested in sex than the wife. For her, at this point in the marriage, it often becomes less a delight and more of a duty of sorts.

Hopefully he is gentle and considerate. And hopefully she won't resent him too much if he is still a bit oversexed. (It just happens that most men are more interested in sex than women). In fact, most women don't really need sex. After the early stages and after kids have come along, the man's approaches may begin to be just a bit too much at times.

Hopefully she won't resent him. Perhaps she can graciously do her wifely duties, and if his advances are not as welcome as before, he may himself become less interested in sex.

I know that what I am about to say goes against what all the conventional "sex experts" have to say. And it probably goes against all the girl talk and locker room talk, but I know what I am saying is true. Once a couple has been married a long time and have had their fill of youthful pleasures, raised a family and now have reached a dignified middle or retirement age--they can be perfectly happy with less sex, and frankly even without sex.

They can be very, very good friends, share memories, go for walks and vacations together, walk hand and hand along the beach, and cuddle warmly in bed together without always having to add sex to the equation.

Sex is just sex. And sex in marriage can be just plain sex and does not necessarily have to be super romantically charged and augmented.

It's not that big of a deal. If you try to make too much of it or expect too much, it will just lead to disappointment, frustration, abuse, and even impotency. Here's a little poem I wrote on this subject:

Sex

It's fun when you're young,
But less wilder and milder,
With each turn of the page
As you mellow with age.
Appreciate each other
And stop looking at another.
Grow older gracefully,
Love each other faithfully,
Stop focusing on your plumbing
And look at the sunset.
It's stunning.

The point is: sex does not need to be embellished, and there is no need for smoke and mirrors. It's plenty fun when you are young. But there comes a time when you're tired, the kids are cranky, or you've got to get up early, when "not tonight, dear" is exactly right.

Sex with love will be less frequent, but it will be more satisfying.

There is nothing wrong with just plain sex in marriage. But sex with love is even nicer.

The love aspect is involved in this way. For her, love is involved by not resenting her husband and by occasionally doing her wifely duty for the sake of her husband's needs, even if she is just going through the motions.

For him, love is involved by being respectful and considerate of her needs and by loving her as a person and not as a sex object. He must always be gentle and kind. He must be willing to say no to his needs out of consideration for her.

For the lady, love mostly means not resenting her husband. But for the man, more is required.

For men, sex is a physical thing. For her, perhaps more mental and emotional. Men tend to have a bigger appetite and are ready to go at the drop of a hat. He must learn to appreciate the difference in appetite. He must be thoughtful and considerate of her needs. He must not force himself upon her. He must be tender and kind, and not pressure her.

As the years go by, and after having enjoyed the early years of marital bliss, kids come along and the man must begin to slowly transcend his selfishness.

Growing in grace, dignity and wisdom, he becomes less animal, less male, and gradually becomes more fatherly.

- 9 -

Sex in Marriage – The Shocking Truth

I already talked about marital sexual relations in the previous chapter, but I'm going to cover this subject one more time to add an exclamation point to what I already said.

The truth is that sex is not that important. Way too much is made of it--to the point that we have the notion that sex has to have Fourth of July fireworks all the time until age 90.

This misconception has led to more unhappiness, resentment, impotency, divorce and infidelity than you can imagine.

The popular but erroneous concept that marriage is to get our needs met, when combined with an incessant focus on sex, has done a lot of harm. How?

Because otherwise reasonably happy couples, with a nice lifestyle, good kids, and a tranquil home, start to become convinced by urban myths, media hype, pop psychology, catty girlfriends, and even misguided Christian advisors that their marriage must be somehow unfulfilling because bells and whistles are not going off five nights a week.

You end up with men with wandering eyes wondering if the grass would be greener with someone else, struggling with some erectile dysfunction drug, or trying to get their needs met with some virtual images.

Society ends up with many women reading romance novels, always trying harder to please, and feeling somehow inadequate.

The idea of getting our needs met, when it permeates society, results in a nation of partners who are just perpetually vaguely dissatisfied.

All of which can lead to unhappiness, extramarital affairs, broken homes, divorces, financial ruin, and the kids being hurt.

Five years after a breakup, one or both partners are still unhappy or even unhappier. Looking back, they arrive at the sad realization that they had it all and threw it all away.

Just who are these strangers who talk so pompously and cavalierly on camera, in the advertisements, in books and in the magazines--who egg us on from stage left to be dissatisfied and demand more and more pleasure?

And just where did the notion that marriage is for getting our needs met come from?

One thing is sure: confusion abounds because of misdirection, wrong ideas, and misguided advice.

So let's state a couple of things that you are not likely to hear, except from a good grandma or good great grandma.

First of all, the purpose of sex is not pleasure. It is for starting and building a family. Children are a blessing from God, and it is for the procreation of children that we are given sex by our Creator.

Of course, He attached pleasure to it. I am not a prude. I understand that it can be fun and pleasurable. God is the one who designed it. It was His idea.

It has its place like any other pleasure. For example, we also derive pleasure from eating. But as the old saying goes--we should "eat to live, not live to eat." Work has a modest pleasure associated with it, but there is more to life than just work. So it is with sex. It has its place within the bounds of holy matrimony. It has its pleasure too.

A couple meet, have a courtship (and it should be a chaste one), and get married. Then they have the pleasure of the marriage bed. It is good that they enjoy each other, and before you know it, kids come along.

But after the first few years of marriage and with a family established, other things become more important, such as parenting, working, maturing, and making some contribution to the good of society.

In fact, marriage is a framework within which to work out our differences and to learn to be unselfish.

There comes a time when sex is just not that important. A husband and wife can then become very good friends, share many wonderful times being together--like going for a walk, enjoying the kids and then grand kids, and working and helping others. They can enjoy holding hands and cuddling, or the warmth and coziness of simply lying side by side. But it does not always have to end in you know what.

It is not true that women need sex. And though men tend to be more sexually oriented than women, men eventually don't need it either.

In fact, men should become more fatherly as the years go by. Less beastly, less juvenile, and more noble.

Less selfish, and more considerate and respectful of her needs.

A couple can be perfectly happy and perfectly fulfilled without sex. (Or with less sex but enjoying it more because it is with love, tenderness and understanding).

I understand that a sexless marriage can result from one or both being resentful. It can also result from one or both placing too much emphasis on performance-- which can make a man feel nervous, self conscious, inadequate, or even impotent.

It can happen when one side is withholding affection because of resentment.

In such cases, the situation can often be solved by simply realizing that resentment is the blocking factor, and letting go of the resentment.

There are also situations where a wife has been abused by other men in the past and develops an aversion to sex or to her husband, because sex reminds her of what happened before.

The husband, realizing that this is the case, must patient and thoughtful. There is a good chance that his decency, gentleness, and thoughtfulness will help her to see that he is not like those other men.

The above exceptions notwithstanding, I still maintain that sex can and should become less and less important as the years pass. I also maintain that the golden years can have wonderful intimacy, sharing, and deep marital friendship without sex.

I will go over the ground one more time, and keep it simple.

First of all, people tend to think that either sex issues or money issues are the reason for unhappiness in marriage. But I can tell you that the sex or money are just handy substitutes for what is going on underneath.

I can tell you that the unhappiness is more likely to be a symptom of resentment, anger, and the subsequent cascade of negative emotions, notions, and actions that ensue. Resentment, judgment, and secret hostility are the real culprits, not unfulfilling sex or money troubles.

Secondly, if a husband and wife love each other and grow in affection and friendship, then after the children have come along sex becomes less and less important, and eventually not important at all. It can be an occasional expression of mutual affection and closeness. But so is walking hand in hand, sitting side by side on the sofa in front of the fire, enjoying family gatherings, or sharing memories and new things to do.

I recently heard a very nice man and a famous Christian author talk about his experience with depression. At one point he said that he was seeking to find more of "those happy moments in life when you don't feel guilty and nothing is required of you."

This is a wonderful insight.

Remember those carefree moments of childhood or youth, when you could just be yourself? When you were not guilty (or being made to feel guilty) and nothing was required of you?

Therefore, dear married partners, I hereby give you permission to relax and not make too big a deal of sex.

Live life intuitively and spontaneously, not according what some stranger says you should be doing.

Enjoy each other and don't try to make anything happen. Incidentally, I know of several people who were trying to have a child with no success. No sooner did they adopt one and stop trying too hard, then-- voila--soon there were two!

Enjoy the delights of the honeymoon and the morning of your marriage. Grow older gracefully and become very good friends.

- *10* -

How to Forgive and Forget

Remember Ann Landers? She was the famous advice columnist who had a daily column in hundreds of newspapers from coast to coast. People sent her troubling personal problems. She gave advice, often quite good.

I'll never forget something she said. Near the end of her long and illustrious career, she was interviewed by someone who asked her: After all your years of giving advice, if you could give people just one piece of advice—what would it be?

Being in the advice business myself, I could not wait to hear her response. She thought about it for a moment and then responded: "If I could give people just one piece of advice, it would be to be more forgiving."

She had seen too many relationships and families destroyed by resentment, unforgiveness, and grudges.

She had seen too many people destroyed by bitterness and unhappiness, the result of not forgiving another. Her advice: Be more forgiving.

All I can say is "amen." If a person were to set out to ruin their own life, there would be no "better" way than through harboring resentment against others.

Resentment (hatred), you see, is a big trauma for a human being. We were never meant to hate. We were created in the image and likeness of God. We are creatures of love. When we are patient with others, our Heavenly Father is patient with us. When we forgive others He forgives us.

When we do not judge and do not resent, we remain in His good graces and we enjoy His love and warmth.

Just like the plant lives in the sun and gets its life from the sun, so the human soul was made to live in God's light. When we resent another, we cut ourselves off from His love. When you resent, you can actually feel the negativity and emptiness.

Resentment is a very big trauma. It forms a memory that sticks in your craw. Worse yet, resentment and hatred cut us off from our own good.

It is true that others can be cruel or mean, others can be confusing, and others make mistakes. But when we resent them, we lose patience with them. This negative energy of impatience and hostility then sustains the fallen ego that lives apart from God and experiences conflict with God.

I must also say a word about judgment. If many men are guilty of anger, then many women are guilty of judgment. In fact, many women say "I never resent anyone." But the issues, negative moods and even health problems they are experience belie their putative innocence.

They are judging others—their husband, their kids, and other people. Judgment is playing God. It is puffing

101

up and judging or condemning another. Men tend to be so weak and wrong, that they make themselves very tempting to judge. Their wrongness permits the woman to judge him with a superior hate. Comparing herself to his animalness and to his weakness or violence, she can feel very superior indeed.

Then she turns around and in order to get rid of the guilt serves him (and others) out of guilt. She can feel like quite the hard done by martyr serving her brood of ungrateful subjects, and even appear saintly in comparison to their grossness and ingratitude.

She keeps doing for them, and they keep getting worse. She quickly absolves herself of the condemnation of her conscience for her sneaky judgments, and never sees her own wrongness through ever comparing herself.

The husband feels very inferior to her saintliness. And the kids either worship her or resent her for her perfection and never admitting that she is wrong.

Therefore, if you are suffering from a variety of symptoms and issues, and things in your life are not getting better, then look for resentment and judgment.

Both are almost guaranteed to be there somewhere. Repent of them.

We think we have a right to judge and resent. We think we can get away with resenting. But we only reap what we sow. When we exercise our right to hate another, we are doing a terrible thing.

It is unfair to the other person. It tempts them to resent us and to judge us back. They are tempted to judge our judgment, in other words.

Being cut off from life devastates our own being.

Many of us were abused, rejected, mistreated or traumatized when we were young. Our being was devastated, and some of us have never fully recovered.

We went out in the world seeking love to fill the emptiness. We used people, food, substances and distractions. But none satisfied. When they did not, we felt betrayed, resented them, and then felt all the more empty.

Others of us were not really mistreated or abused and yet we too felt empty, loveless, and went out into the world looking for love. There we discovered abuse.

Why is it that we become so empty and feel so unloved? Why are we so needy that we grovel before others for a few crumbs of approval or settle for the most lowly and sometimes loathsome substitutes for love?

It is not what others did to us. Nor is it because of what we were denied or thought we were denied. It is because we became resentful and judgmental.

Resentment cuts us off from our connection to God within. Resentment cuts us off from the wellspring of good to which we have access when we are not resentful. Judgment permits us to feel right in comparison to those we are judging.

It was our own resentment that hurt us more than anything. We feel empty and we then blame those who did something to us. But blame only reinforces and adds another layer of resentment, keeping us apart from our Creator. Whether we blame others or turn the blame on ourselves, blame is a way of justifying our pride. All it does is keep us tied to bitter memories and cut off from the healing balm of God's love.

Our need for human love is to fill the emptiness from not having God's love. That is why what we call love often ends up in fighting and hurt feelings. What we call love is a substitute for the agape, emotionless love we all need.

This emotionless love would correct our childish need for love. True love corrects us of our need for the love from others that does not fulfill. True love sets us free from our neediness. And when we no longer need love, we can give love. And when we found the love of the Father it would immunize us from hurting or being hurt by others.

Remember what Christ said: "If you forgive others, your Heavenly Father will forgive you. But if you do not forgive others, He will not forgive you." Therefore, I would like you to consider watching for resentment in yourself. When you see it, stand back and let it pass.

You will be glad you did. By learning to be patient with others, you will find the love from God welling up inside you.

Therefore, dear ladies, forgive your father for not being there for you; and then do not resent your husband. If he is decent, then appreciate his good qualities. If he does not have the mysterious emotionless corrective love, then simply do not resent him. You will then be able to receive the love from your Creator within.

Husbands, do not look to your wives for love. Instead of looking for love, have love for others. And if, through soul searching, yearning and seeking the wisdom you do not have, you should find an inner rapport with your Creator, you will then be able to share such love with others. It will not be your love, but the love of God coming through you.

- 11 -

How to Apologize and Clear the Air with Dignity

I recently got this question. It will serve as a good example of the difference between apologizing and saying you are sorry vs. asking someone to forgive you. Never say "Can you forgive me?" I will explain. First, let's read the question I got.

"Dear Pastor Roland,
 Should I ask her to forgive me?"

"I am 47 years old. I'm cleaning up my act--I've stopped drinking and smoking dope like I used to. I've been divorced for 7 years (I can see now that it was mainly my fault) and I have 3 kids, all grown now. We exchange cards at Christmas time, but communication is not good.

I spend a lot of time pondering my past. I read the Bible, and when I'm at work (I'm a truck driver) I do a lot of thinking about the past.

Pastor Roland, I was not a very nice person when I was younger. Without going into details, I hurt a lot of people. Now I see that I was wrong and I'm sorry.

There are at least three or four people I want to apologize to. Should I just leave them alone or should I go to them and ask them to forgive me?"
Jason

Here is my answer.

Dear Jason,

I am glad that you can see now that you were wrong and I am glad that you are sorry. I can tell that it is genuine.

If possible, it is good to apologize to someone you did wrong. Sometimes it is not possible: they are dead or you don't know where they are. Or they do not want anything to do with you. If so, then just be sorry in your heart and move forward with your life.

But if the door is open a little, then it is can be helpful to the other person.

If your apology is sincere (and I am sure that yours will be), then it relieves them of unfinished business.

One of the most difficult things that we all have to deal with is when someone has done us wrong, but they refuse to admit they are wrong, or they pretend that nothing happened. It is a great temptation for us to keep resenting them. It makes it hard to get closure.

But when that person admits what he did and apologizes, then we can now let go of our resentment.

We no longer have an excuse to resent him (since he said he were sorry).

Bear in mind that the people you apologize to may not forgive you. They may want to hold onto their grudge. But now you have cleared the air and made it possible for them to let it go. Whether they do or not is none of your concern. If they do, it is good for them. If they don't, it's bad for them. But never mind. You did your job by clearing the air.

If you can say you are sorry in person, it is more powerful than on the phone or in a letter. If the other person does not want to see you, and you can send a letter (without being intrusive), then send a letter saying you are sorry for what you did.

Just be careful because some people are not sincere and they will use anything you say against you. Use discretion. (This is also true when it comes to husbands who made some mistakes but now see the light. If you confess every detail of your errors, all you are doing is tempting her to judge you. Keep it simple. Say "I have not been the man I should have been and you needed. I apologize and am sorry, but from now on things will be different." That's all you need to say. Now just go about your duties and be that man from now on).

Here is an important point. *Never* say to another person "Can you forgive me?" or "Can you ever forgive me?"

Asking another person to forgive you is a temptation to them.

No one can forgive you except God. God forgives. You are tempting them to play God.

Your one and only job (as the one who did them wrong) is to clear the air--state what you did, apologize, and say you are sorry.

In simple terms--admit you were wrong. Apologize and say you are sorry. Keep it simple. After you have apologized, then take leave. Maybe they will say "no problem." Maybe they will never let it go. Either way it is none of your concern. You have cleared the air.

Whether they stop hating and resenting you or not is between them and their conscience.

By apologizing and being sorry, you have given them a chance to exercise a free will choice: Let go of their grudge or keep hating you. They can let go and be free; or hang on to the hate and continue to deteriorate. It's their choice and none of your concern as to what the outcome is.

Don't pester them or try to have a relationship with them. This is akin to pretending that nothing happened and can tempt them to resent you. Don't require that they like you or want to have something to do with you.

Again, I want to point out the faulty approach that is surprisingly common, but wrong. Never ask another person to forgive you. It actually tempts them to play God. Instead apologize for what you did and say you are sorry. It's that simple.

While I am at it, I want to clear up another misconception that people have. Let's say that you are on the receiving end of being wronged. Many of us have difficulty forgiving (letting go of resentment and a grudge against the person who wronged us) because we think it means that we have to pretend that nothing happened and like them or have something to do with them. But this is not true. You can forgive a person and never have anything to do with them.

For example, you can forgive someone for stealing your stuff and nevertheless call the police and have them arrested. Forgiving means not resenting, not hating, and not judging. It does not mean pretending nothing happened. It does not mean liking them.

The same goes for dealing with members of your family who harmed you. Many of us have had a parent or a relative who did us wrong when we were kids.

There was emotional or physical abuse; or we were neglected or abandoned. The reason we have trouble forgiving them is because we haven't yet dropped our resentment, we haven't confronted them to undo the

108

intimidation, or we fear that we will have to have a relationship with them.

First, by far the most important thing is: let go of the resentment. I've said it before, but I can't repeat it enough, because people have a hard time grasping this critically important principle. Forgiving means dropping resentment.

In fact many of us want to forgive, but we literally do not know how. We think it means crying emotional tears or perhaps making affirmations. We even think that we have to do nice things for the person we had been unforgiving to. But such is not the case.

Forgiveness means no longer resenting and judging.

It's that simple. If you have forgiven someone (dropped your resentment), it won't be long before when you encounter them you will feel absolutely nothing (expect perhaps a mild unemotional compassion).

Even better yet, once you start meditating for objectivity and find the meditative state of mind, you will quickly see that forgiveness also means never having judged someone in the first place. Now that I meditate and am more enlightened, when I see people making errors, I see the errors, *but I just don't resent them for their errors.*

And because I don't resent them, I don't feel guilty. So it is easy to speak up.

Reading my books and practicing my meditation helps. You will become objective and see why you no longer need hang onto resentment. Once you have let it go, you are now in a position where you can confront someone over what they did. And you may need to do this in order to clear the air and to get rid of the intimidation factor.

Undoubtedly in the past, you may have tried to confront them and make them admit what they did, but it did not turn out well. They denied it or blamed you. And this led to another round of resentment.

But this time, if you have meditated with my meditation and read my books, and have had a change of heart about things, you will be able to let go of the resentment because you see that they were victims too.

No longer hating them, you can approach them with love this time (without the resentment). You will be able to say "when I was a child you did bad things to me. You did this and this and this. I hated you. But now I don't hate you anymore. I just want you to know what you did to me and give you a chance to apologize and say you are sorry."

At this point, the person may break down and admit what they did and be sorry about it. Or (most likely) he or she will again deny what they did, accuse you of being ungrateful, being a trouble maker, etc, etc. etc. etc.

At this point you say: "You know my number. When you are ready to apologize and mean it, give me a call."

Then you can walk away with your head held high, shake the dust from your feet and never have anything to do with them again.

At some point, the person may approach, cry and put on a big show about how s/he is suffering and how mean you are being. Watch out for this ploy. He or she is just trying to pull on your heartstrings. The person is not truly sorry, just trying to save their pride by having you take back the truth. If you feel sorry for them and give in, you are back in the trap again. The other person hasn't learned anything and s/he hangs onto their pride and got away with something. Worse yet, you are harming them. Why?

Because unless the person repents and is sorry, there is no hope of that person getting right with conscience and with God. The person remains an enemy of truth and their soul is in mortal danger. By taking back the truth and giving in, you become an enabler of this.

If you give in and let them get away with it, then you are actually hurting them. Think of it--by holding your ground sternly, you are actually being kind! You are giving them a chance to repent. And if they do—just think how good this is for their soul. Your holding up the Light only hurts their pride (and the thing that has made a home in them). You are not really hurting the person, you are giving them a chance to repent.

To recapitulate: you can forgive another person and never have anything to do with them again. You do not have to pretend nothing happened. Something happened, but now you just don't resent them anymore for it. That's all.

You don't have to like them or have anything to do with them. Of course, if they come around and are truly repentant, then you may have a relationship with them, *if you want to*. But you don't have to.

In fact, you can forgive them (in your heart) and then shake the dust off your feet, move on and start a new life and never see them again.

I hope this helps. Pastor Roland

- 12 -

Who Should I Marry?
Courtship and Pre-Marriage Considerations

Many people ask about whether they should marry a certain person or not. With a few exceptions I can never advise on this subject. I am not standing in your shoes. Nor do I know the couple, except perhaps a brief conversation with one of them.

Of course there are times when the other person is a drug addict, a repeat criminal, is still married to someone else, or is promiscuous. In such cases the answer to the question "should I date or marry this person?" is an obvious "not a good idea."

But when it comes to two good people, all I can do is give some general principles. You will have to search your heart and pray.

Generally I advise a young lady to look for a man who has a fire in his belly for justice. A man who loves principle and is willing to stand for something. There is an unmistakable spark of fire there--character, principle, a love of what is right. It's also nice if he is already or in the process of establishing himself in a trade, profession or business.

I tell guys not to look for the perfect woman. Look for a lady who will good naturedly admit it when you point something out.

Don't misunderstand--I am not saying that a woman has to be submissive or be dominated by a man. In fact, if the man is out of order, she should speak up and point it out. In my home, everyone is free to speak up to me. And they do!

I'm just saying that some people are clever at acting meek and mild, but are resentful underneath. Not good.

Some women let him be in charge. She lets him be in charge--even though she is really the one in charge.

Look for someone who is good natured and who respects what is right more than her own ego. She will defer to her man (if he is right).

I am not in favor of casual dating. It is a terrible idea and leads to promiscuity, sexually transmitted diseases and a loss of character. A man who plays the field loses his character. His future wife will know it and will probably secretly judge him for it and hold it against him.

Instead of playing the field, he should be becoming established in business.

A woman who casually dates is putting herself in situations (being alone in a car with a man, for example) that can only lead to a loss of innocence, and even danger.

I am in favor of young people doing wholesome activities in groups (like 2 or 3 guys and 2 or 3 gals going out together in a group). Bowling, skiing, church activities, picnics, bike riding, studying, going to a concert or a move and so on as a group is fun and much safer.

After lots of getting to know the person in these safe group settings, if you think this is the guy then courtship may begin.

I do believe in courtship. This means that when a man and a woman go out to lunch or to a movie, just the two of them, it is with the intention of definitely considering this particular person for marriage and definitely wanting to know if she or he is right. The purpose of the courtship date is to consider this person for marriage. And I also believe in waiting until after the marriage ceremony to consummate the marriage.

I am often asked about marrying someone from another religion or a completely different background. I am not rigid on this matter, because the person himself or herself is most important, not what cultural background or organized religion their family belonged to.

Character and what is in the person's heart are most important--such as honesty and a love of truth. Does the person love children? Is the person kind? There must be no drinking, gambling, or use of drugs (such as marijuana). Also watch out for the man who walks around on egg shells, never corrects anything, and is worshipful of her--he wants something. He is weak and lacks character.

How about someone who is just not religious at all or who doesn't know about God or even care about religion? Well, at least they are not a fanatic. It may work out. In fact I have always said I would rather have a person who is decent and has a good heart, but was raised in a home where religion was not even talked about than someone who has just memorized a bunch of things.

They simply memorize things and conform to a shallow (but usually rigid) knowledge. These people are not true Christians at all even though they say and do all the right things. They give real Christians a bad name.

Many a man marries a woman who "gets saved" and then she lords it over him with smug superiority and is always trying to change him and convert him.

A woman might marry a "religious" man who rigid and hateful underneath. He eventually reveals his cruelty and violence in laying down the law in the name of religion. Run from such types.

Don't misunderstand me. There is a true Christianity which is a seeking soul's gradually finding an inner bond with its Creator. This true Christian would never try to impose himself or herself on anyone. He or she will never manipulate or use pressure. This true Christian realizes what a delicate thing it is to introduce a person to an inner rapport with God.

Bottom line: avoid weak womanizing men. Avoid zealots of all kinds, whether religious, atheists, or political.

Of course, there is the situation where two people marry and neither really thinks much about religion at all. Time passes and gradually and gently, through searching and finding, one makes a commitment to what they know in their heart and discover that their love of truth is really a love of God. This person, in essence, wakes up from their hypnotic slumber in culture and tradition and lies, and begins to see reality (because they now love reality) and love their conscience. This waking up person now finds himself or herself wedded to someone who is not awake and aware.

There is a passage in the Bible where Paul says that if

a lady becomes a follower of Christ and finds herself wedded to an unbeliever, perhaps her goodness and noble demeanor may yet awaken her spouse to truth.

Perhaps he will wake up and maybe he won't. If he does not, it is hard; but it gives her a chance to practice patience.

But this is a far cry from chasing her husband around the house with a Bible, trying to convert him (which will only turn him in her zombie or drive him off to another woman or the bottle).

Since it is the man who is supposed to be the head of household, it is easier if it is he who gradually comes to his Creator first. Then his nobility, his principled nature, and gentle lordship may win the respect of his wife for himself and his God.

It is more difficult for the woman who wakes up and is married to a husband who is not awake. If she tries to convert him, he would only be falling for the temptation she represents. About all she can do is do her duty, be gracious, kind, patient and noble--and her light may wake him up. If it does, he will either hate that light and probably leave her, or he will love the light and then they can be very good friends.

Perhaps now you can see why I cannot advise from the distance about any particular person. I know in my life the people I have been drawn to and felt comfortable around are seemingly the opposite of what you would expect. There are arranged marriages that work out just fine. There are marriages that fall apart and years later, when both have matured, there is reconciliation.

It is not my job to figure things out. Where I am most helpful is for issues in marriage. People get married, the honeymoon is over, and then issues arise. That is where Pastor Roland can come to the rescue!

But when it comes to finding the right mate, I can't play match maker. All I can do is mention some principles to consider. That's all.

Besides, it all depends on the will of God and what He might have in mind for us.

A man can get married, and like most men, be selfish and immature. He is weak and not there for his wife or kids. He makes a mess out of things and a divorce happens. But he starts to wake up. He realizes he was wrong and selfish and now is ready to be a good husband. Reconciliation is not possible and then he meets a lady and starts a second family. This time he is a good, noble, thoughtful man, but in order to build character, the Lord gives him a family that does not appreciate him and does nothing but give him a hard time. So now instead of suffering for his wrongs, he suffers for righteousness sake. It's no fun, but he learns to be a man and his character grows.

Most of us, if not all of us, get married for the wrong reasons. Once married, often seemingly to the wrong person, we have to get back to basics and learn how to be unselfish. Marriage is not a picnic. It was not meant to be. It is a framework ordained by God in which to work out our differences and learn to be unselfish.

When all is said and done, it is a mystery to me how people find each other and then end up married. In absolute terms it is good to marry someone who you think is the right person. It is nice to be with someone you have a lot in common with and who you feel comfortable with.

Just be aware that the nice person may not be the best for you. It is a woman's job to give a man a hard time. Her hard time is a chance for him to demonstrate patience and understanding. The more unreasonable she is, the more reasonable he must be. It can have a happy ending, but only if the man quickly matures and demonstrates the patience of Job and the Wisdom of Solomon.

A wise man once said there can be no courage without danger. Similarly, there can be no character without a test of that character.

Marriage is not to get our needs met. It is to bring children into the world.

So I must say that for the man, it almost doesn't matter who he marries as far as character growth is concerned. It is his job to be a man and to have patience, courage, longsuffering, kindness, nobility and honor. The worse she is, the more he will suffer. But if he suffers rightly, he will grow in character and shine.

For the lady, it is good if she can find a man who is principled and honorable. Definitely she should stay away from the weak ladies man. She should also stay away from the violent type. It helps if she has a good father, because then she will look for a man like her father.

There are some practical concerns. A guy might be nice, but if he does not want kids and you do--there is not much hope in such an arrangement. If he is too close to a mother who rules him emotionally and mentally, and who views you (the wife) as a threat to her power--it will be rough sledding.

If you want the kids to be Christian and she doesn't or he doesn't or if you want to home school the kids but he does not. Again, caution.

I have put a lot on the table. Some of what I say are hard teachings. But do not do something just because I say so or anyone else says so. Hear what I say and what others say, but then pray and trust your God given intuition. It is okay to read what I write, but just don't put me (or anyone else) on a pedestal.

There are some really excellent values questionnaires, programs and seminars put out by Christian organizations. And many local pastors offer couples classes for courtship and for newly weds. I'm in favor of attending and benefiting from these programs and classes. Just don't get too caught up in analyzing, over planning and endlessly second guessing yourself. Have faith. Trust what you know in your heart.

My wife and I met and had ice cream at an ice cream parlor near college and within 6 months we were married. I didn't know then what I know now. Back then I was just as starry eyed as any other young person.

But I've grown and learned a lot. Marriage is good for us. Before marriage, we can be self centered and get away with it. Marriage is a framework within which to grow and learn to be unselfish.

People get married and enjoy each other during the honeymoon and the spring of their marriage. But it isn't long before issues arise. When they do, it's time for some basic training about life, marriage and the nature of men and women. So when it is time, get married and enjoy each other.

Then when issues arise, get Pastor Roland's books for the instructions.

Blessings. Pastor Roland

- 13 -

A Deeper Look Into Relationship Dynamics

A listener asked: Does Divorce affect the kids? Roland takes the opportunity to discuss the deeper aspects of relationships.

Roland answers the question, but then gives us a profound and eye opening insight into the man woman dynamic. (Editor)

Bottom line: divorce is worse for the kids than their seeing you arguing. There are exceptions, of course, but divorce is a big and deep trauma for kids. Best to avoid it–if possible.

I must first lay some groundwork, so here goes. If you are sincere about salvaging your relationship with your spouse and want the best for the kids, then please hear me out.

What I say may at first sound old fashioned. But if you can read calmly, you may begin to see tried and true principles have survived for a good reason—they work.

Look--I love men, women and kids, and I believe that the family is the foundation of society. I would like to see people living happily ever after. So my tough love is meant to awaken you to your senses.

Does divorce affect the kids? The short answer is "of course it does." If someone thinks it doesn't, they are fooling themselves. In a popular article I wrote I made reference to the excellent book *The Unexpected Legacy of Divorce: a 25 Year Landmark Study*. But you don't have to read the book to know that divorce affects the kids. All you have to do is look around you or look into your own life to see that it does.

Of course, there is always the situation where one partner is such a terrible person that divorce is inevitable. For example, the children must be protected from a drug addict, a violent person, or a molester.

But for the most part, divorce takes place between two good people. It is a divorce based on misunderstanding, hurt feelings, a desire to escape from commitment, or in the notion of "having my needs met." Divorce is often a way of getting even, or perhaps of distancing oneself from a situation.

In other words, it is based in selfishness, immaturity and resentment. If the two good people involved could get some good old fashioned advice, grow up a little, and be more forgiving—divorce does not have to happen.

I am not in favor of divorce. Sometimes a temporary separation may be needed for a cooling off period or to give everyone some space. For example, even sleeping in different rooms for a little while sometimes helps.

Sometimes one person's behavior has been egregious, but he or she can be given another chance. A period of separation is needed (without marriage perks) to give that person one last chance to clean up their act before beginning relations again on proper terms.

But sometimes one or both parties are just looking for an excuse to get away and escape from dealing with the situation. Often this rationale (excuse) is used: "it is better to divorce than for the kids to see us arguing all the time."

Kids can deal with arguing (if it doesn't deteriorate in violence, drinking and so on). But divorce is a big trauma for them that is harder to cope with than parents arguing.

That is one of the reasons why I have written this book. By gaining a deeper understanding of what is involved when two people come together, you may be able to heal your hurt, become a better person, and perhaps heal your relationship.

As the adult child of a broken relationship, your understanding the inherited legacy we all share from Adam and Eve will permit you to not replay your parents' mistakes in your relationship to infect the next generation.

Through understanding and a sincere desire to do what is right, the reader may be able to forgive their partner and become less selfish. Moreover, the children and adult children of failing parents may find understanding and forgiveness that will permit them to not become victims of the legacy themselves.

I believe that if the children of troubled marriages can find a way not to resent their parents, they can be free to become happy and balanced adults--one day spouses and parents, without having to bring the baggage of the past into the future.

I believe that kids who now resent their parents (or who have resented their parents) can, with a little understanding, begin to forgive their parents. I believe that if they do drop their grudges, and if they become friends with their conscience, they will recover from the trauma of having resented their parents. They will be able to leave the sad legacy of dysfunctionality behind and be free to become good parents themselves.

Divorce is a symptom of error, misunderstanding, and resentment. In order to get beyond the blame game stage, we must discover what causes the errors, misunderstanding, and resentment.

So, fasten your seatbelt. Here goes.

Let's take a deeper look into the dynamics that take place in a relationship and separate them out so you can see how one thing leads to another.

I think we can all agree that divorce is not a good thing. No matter how society tries to make it seem like it is no big deal, it is a big deal. Therefore, it would be best to avoid it. However, again I must say that I am writing to basically good people.

Obviously there are always situations where one partner is a terrible, terrible person. I don't think the other partner should sacrifice his or her life in order to stay with an alcoholic, a violent person, a drug addict or an abusive person. Nor should the children be put in jeopardy.

Generally, for self protection and the protection of the kids, it's best to be as far away from the terrible person as possible. When crime and violence are involved, you should do whatever we can within the bounds of the law and morality, including using the full force of the law, if necessary, to protect yourself and the innocent kids. Just as we sometimes need to use the services of a doctor, so there are times when we need to use the services of an attorney, social services or local law enforcement.

If you are in danger and afraid for yourself and your kids, you need professional help. If you are afraid to take the steps needed, then find someone in your family or among your friends who is emotionally strong and who will go with you and help you. If your kids are in any kind of danger, it is your responsibility to protect them.

With all the drugs, abuse, pornography, crime, and terrible things that people get involved in today, and with all the multiple partners and complex things that go on, I just can't deal with them here or sort things out for you.

What I can do is talk in general spiritual principles so that you can see how the error and suffering begin, and why society is in trouble and families are falling apart.

If you get a firm grasp on sound principles, begin to drop resentments and grudges, and begin to see things objectively, you will, with the help of God, be able to eventually sort things out for yourself.

The terrible situations, the divorces, the family and societal ills and the suffering are due to something called sin. And because America is more in rebellion against God and His right way today than ever before, the horrors are going to mount until we as a people individually and collectively repent and turn from error.

There is a passage in the Old Testament about what happened to a land where "everyone did what was right in their own eyes," and the result was destruction. Isn't that what we have today? Everyone is doing his or her own thing. We live rebellious, hedonistic, immoral or amoral lives, pursuing what we want and what makes us feel good. We are selfish and willful. Many people are haughty, phony, naughty, and will not take correction.

They take this attitude into their relationship.

And so, being ambitious and willful, resentful and selfish, we are easily misled by people who promise us what we want. And when we follow them, we are led into error. We then look for someone or something to accept us just as we are and comfort us. They comfort us in our wrong, thus permitting us to stay wrong.

Unless we wake up and cry out to God for answers, we will be compelled to keep living wrongly, believing wrong advice, and ending up in even worse shape.

124

Today the family and the individual are in worse shape that ever. You see wall to wall sickness, suffering, chaos and ruination everywhere. We as a nation have been seduced. We were seduced to sin. And when we did, we became subject to the god of sin, the one who wants you to be his servant.

In order to become your master, he first tempted you to step away from the straight and narrow—such as a little puff of marijuana, a little resentment, a little promiscuity, and a little indulgence here or there.

Someone probably tried to warn you. Your parents may have warned you about drugs, but you wanted to be accepted at school, and you probably bought the lie that "marijuana is harmless."

You started dating. A concerned minister or grandma may have tried to warn you about casual dating. But you thought they were old fashioned.

Your friends may have even tried to warn you about some guy. They said: "Don't go out with that guy, he's no good." But you didn't want to listen.

Your parents and other authorities tried to warn you about marijuana, alcohol, premarital sex, or spending too much money. They may have tried to warn you about being selfish, wanting your own way, ignoring your parents and so on.

But each step of the way someone or a permissive voice in your head was beckoning you to "express yourself." All too often, so-called friends, the pop culture, music and song lyrics, college professors, experts and media people all cater to egos by saying that you should do your own thing. Some may have said it was "your right." And so, you began to succumb.

No sooner did you indulge anything your parents said not to do or that you knew in your heart was not right, than you felt uneasy.

Instead of admitting your error and reconciling with conscience, you looked for support in the world. And the very ones who enticed you to stray in the first place now provided the comfort to reassure you. If you got a sexually transmitter disease, they had a shot or pills for it. The remedy may have worked for awhile. But before long the physical, emotional, and spiritual consequences of error evolved to the point where there was no quick fix. Even some acquired diseases such as Aids or herpes are manageable but generally not curable.

Always we are looking for the way to do whatever we want without consequences. So they declare some things to be "a disease," not a sin, so as to remove guilt.

Perhaps they declare something to be genetic (so you don't have to accept responsibility for a misdirected lifestyle). Sometimes they try to come up with a vaccine, so everyone can go on thumbing their nose at God's commandments and not have to pay any price.

Now do you see what is wrong with no fault divorce?

It is too easy. It is a way out for anyone who is selfish, who doesn't want to honor their commitment, or who wants to play the field. It is also an out for someone who is resentful, vindictive, judgmental and full of unforgiveness. It is an out for people who are totally selfish and not getting their needs met, or who are willful and resent their partners for not bowing to their will.

Those who encourage you to divorce are, for the most part, enablers. They are catering to your ego. They see what you want—an excuse to indulge yourself in some selfish pleasure, an easy out, an escape, a chance to get even, or to cop out on a commitment—and they say that it is okay. By making it easy, they make it so you never have to face your own selfishness.

The spirit of the lie itself comes to the aid of the selfish egotist. It whispers the words our ego wants to hear: "your kids will be better off not seeing you arguing, you are giving her freedom to find herself, you've grown apart, she doesn't understand you, no one will get hurt, etc. etc." In our egotistical state, the lie always seems warm and understanding; whereas truth seems harsh and cold.

Who tells you to stick it out and suffer? Who tells you to do your duty and not become resentful because you are not getting your needs met? Who tells you that if you let go of resentment and judgment, you might see that your spouse is not a bad person?

I was listening to a well known Christian family advice program on the radio today. The co-hosts devoted 3 half hour programs to exploring how unhappy a certain wife was because her husband was a workaholic. Incidentally, I bet there are many wives who wished they had that problem! She admitted that he made plenty of money, they had good kids, a beautiful home, and he was gentle and kind. He even stood by her for 3 years when she was sick and unable to function.

So what is her problem? She gives him a hard time every chance she has because he is not there for her.

As usual, the well known counselors focused away from the key issue. They focused on how she could go about trying to get his attention, so that she can convince him he needs to change, and then how to change him.

But they are missing the boat. The elephant in the living room is: she resents her husband. This resentment is poisoning and tainting everything. The counselors are taking her side, and thus subtly condoning her resentment and judgment by not pointing it out.

She is basically correct in her assessment, but wrong about what she thinks the cure is. I'm rather sure she is correct that he is not there for her. She is trying to make him aware of this fact. But she thinks that if he were around more and they did more together – that would be the cure; or if he paid more attention to her romantically and emotionally, that would be the cure.

I can categorically tell you, without any hesitation, that if her husband were to change: become a lovey dozy, flower and chocolate bringing husband who attends to her every need—she would not be happy either.

Especially if he were home so much, he stopped working and she had to go to work!

Therefore, I can also safely say that although the problem is basically *his* fault—the solution is in her hands. The solution to this problem is not his just being home more or paying more attention to her. The solution is letting go of her resentment and judgment.

Why? Because even if he were home all the time, attentive to her every whim, he would still not be there for her! What she needs from him—though she does not know herself just what she needs--is an emotionless love. It is an agape corrective love that is from the Father. It can come through the husband, but it is not from the husband. It is from God. And this emotionless love is what we all need.

Her husband may never find it, so she can't wait for him. She has to stop resenting him and then she can find the emotionless agape love within.

My heart goes out to her, because it is basically her husband's fault. But I have to say that whether he ever finds what he is now missing or not, she can still recover her peace of mind and joy if she can let go of her resentment and judgment.

She must not let the state of her soul and emotional well being depend on whether he finds himself or not.

He may never find himself. But if she lets go of the resentment and judgment, she can find God's love welling up inside.

She will be fulfilled and the void will be filled. By not resenting, she becomes unblocked from discovering God's love.

You see, the truth is that it is the Father we have never known that we are seeking. If the love from God can come through her husband, that would be nice. If not, it does not matter. She can find it within when she is willing to give up her willfulness and judgment.

He, on the other hand, needs to see what *being there* really means. Because if he were *really there* for her, the problem would also be solved.

So here goes. First let me address you husbands.

What your family needs is the father spirit. A man must have a bond with the Father Within.

He must make principle more important than anything, even his wife. He must love principle (what he knows in his heart is right) more than anything. Such a man has an inner bond with God. And this is known by way of a love of truth, and by being close to intuition and conscience.

It is an inner bond between his soul and the Light of Truth. For this reason, a man can go to church, read the Bible, volunteer, be an attentive husband and father, and do all the right things, and yet not have this inner bond.

You cannot find this inner rapport through study. It only can happen through yearning for truth with all your heart, and having a burning desire to know the truth. It can only happen through a love of principle and a willingness to sacrifice perks and privileges for what is right. It comes by standing for what is right, come what may.

This type of man, standing for what is right with his human strength, is noted by God. And at some point, the man's yearning for truth and willingness to stand for principle is met by the compassion of the Father Who begin to draw His child back to Himself.

It is the Father Spirit that our wives and children need to see in us men.

I will never forget something I once read. It was about the life of a sea captain who lived in the 1800's.

The story related how despite the fact that this sea captain was at sea for months at a time, his wife and his daughter respected and loved him dearly. Moreover, they were happy and secure, though he was thousands of miles away. They knew he was a man of the highest honor and impeccable virtue. He was a noble, principled man doing his duty. And they loved him for his goodness. They loved him for what he stood for. He had the father spirit.

It is an inner bond. His family saw it in him, and though he was far away, they felt secure and loved. Love is a powerful force. This noble man was "there for them" though physically far away.

I have to say that some of us have had so much religion imposed on us from outside, that it interferes and replaces the inner bond. You cannot study your way to God. Religious study is just another substitute and replacement for the inner bond.

This does not mean that we should not read the Bible. But when we read, it should awaken us to realize the meaning, the reality, behind the words. Moreover, to realize the Presence of the Spirit that is quietly testifying within to the truth of the words on the page.

When we realize, we are experiencing the testimony of the inner Spirit. It is the Spirit that testifies to the truth of what you are reading. All the external words do is possibly awaken you to the inner testimony.

It is this inner testimony, a light shining and wordlessly making you aware of something, which is the important thing. This inner relationship, which may become an inner bond with the Spirit within, is your most prized possession.

Without it, you remain an externalized creature.

Without it the words are dead ("the letter killeth, but the Spirit giveth life"). Without the inner Spirit, we remain dead in our sins. That is why study, especially religious study, can be deadly. Too much study fixates a person to the outside and renders him or her unaware of the wordless Word within.

Christ said: "Of myself, I can do nothing. It is the Father within Who doth the works."

God is the Source of Life, of love, true motivation, of wisdom, knowledge, of true science, mathematics and true art. That is why all true creativity and discovery come from intuition. They come from inside, from the inner light and spirit—from God.

The external fact, for example, bears witness to the truth that was made true by God. And when you see that a fact is true (such as one plus one equals two), you are seeing it in the inner Light from God. The inner light testifies wordlessly to the truth of the fact.

And the fact on the outside bears witness to the inner truth and to the Creator of all truth.

All true scientists, explorers, artists, and leaders tap into something within from which they are inspired.

Einstein, Tesla, Columbus, Moses, David, Paul, Thomas Edison, Mozart, and George Washington all had this inner inspiration.

We must all be like them. Christ had the complete and perfect inner bond with the Father Within. Thus He was the Master of everything. His every word was inspired and had life. His words brought salvation and hope to all who heard and believed. People who were receptive to Him were awakened to see the Father Spirit in Him and to the inner testimony of the Spirit within themselves. Believing deeply, they were saved and healed of all manner of afflictions.

He was the master scientist, turning water into wine, feeding the 5000, and quieting the storm and waves. He was the master physician, healing the sick and raising the dead.

He had complete mastery of knowledge. He thoroughly grasped the scripture. He knew in advance what was to come, and he knew about people's lives (such as the woman at the well) before they told him.

Scientists and statesman, such as Einstein or Washington, are, to some extent, close to the inner fount from which comes intuition. They are close to the inner light, the source of inspiration, because of their love of truth or their emotionless love for others.

More specifically, they have a disinterested love of truth, of others, or of principle, (which is close to loving God, even if they don't consciously realize it).

They love truth for its own sake, without any desire for ego benefit.

To the extent that the mathematician loves truth, he is closer to God than the one who doesn't. To the extent that a person remains in touch with inspiration from within, he or she will bring forth some new facet of truth.

To the extent that a naturalist, botanist, or zoologist loves some aspect of nature, he or she is closer to God (if that love also awakens to a sense of awe and wonder for the Creator of nature).

Just as with knowledge, any endeavor or discovery is good as long as it includes an awareness of God.

Knowledge alone, without understanding, is dangerous and lop sided.

Incidentally, conscience means "with knowing." Conscience means doing something with knowing—in other words with awareness, by which we realize the rightness or the trueness of something.

Please try to track with me, because this has everything to do with the role of father or husband. I am laying some groundwork so that you might see what I mean.

There are two ways to do anything. One way is like an animal, without awareness, without really seeing the meaning of the moment. We have all had the experience of standing before some authority who applied some rule arbitrarily. It pained us because they did not have heart. They didn't understand.

Those moments in life when we ourselves made some big mistake were usually moments when we set aside conscience and awareness. We were either all caught up in emotion, or we set conscience aside because we made something we wanted too important.

For example, two scientists might be doing research. One is operating without awareness and is busy creating bio weapons. The other has awareness and sees the meaning of what he is doing. His research is finding a way to help people live longer.

One employee is just going through the motions of repairing a car in order to get it over with and go home.

Another employee sees the big picture and is working with awareness of what it all means. He sees a safety issue and tells the car owner so it can be fixed, even though it means he has to work a little longer.

Even a ballerina, cook, carpenter, musician, or an athlete is bringing forth a talent and love given to them by God. Whether they know it or not, whether they appreciate it or not, and whether they then use it for good or not.

To the extent that we reject the truth, we fall away from intuition. To the extent that someone on the outside seduces or pressures us to pursue another calling than the one prepared for us by God, we fall away from God.

To the extent that we listen to external experts instead of what we know within, we fall away from God.

This does not mean that we should not hear what they say. Go ahead and listen to what people say, but just don't accept what they say mindlessly. Run what they say by conscience. If something is true or is really helpful, it should sit right with your intuition.

To the extent that we doubt what we know in our heart, we become separated from it.

Likewise, when we make anything more important than our attentiveness to the rightness of things, we become separated from the inner way.

Gentlemen, can you now see why making your wife's, kid's or anyone else's approval too important separates you from a bond with your true ground of being?

That's why you must not be there to win a popularity contest. (Let me quickly add, however, that this does not mean you can be a dictator--because if you had a real bond with intuition, it would give you grace, kindness, patience, and understanding).

The role of Rhett Butler in the classic movie *Gone with the Wind* was played by the dashing, handsome Hollywood idol Clark Gable. In one of his most famous scenes, after a long argument the leading lady gave him a hard time about something. He replied with perhaps his most quoted and famous line when he turned to her and said: "Frankly, my Dear, I don't give a damn."

A real man must have a "don't give a damn" attitude when it comes to his wife's or anyone else's opinions about what he sees is right. A man of vision sees what is right and has the courage of conviction to follow through, even if the whole world is arrayed against him.

Of course, he really has to be really be right.

It is a wife's job to tempt him to doubt himself. Any "good" Eve worth her salt will test him severely. And should he be tested and found not wanting, he will win the prize of her respect. If he wimps out, he will get her sympathy, but earn her contempt.

Do you remember the famous movie *High Noon*? In the movie, the hero, played by Gary Cooper, had just resigned as sheriff so he could get married and move away to be a rancher. This was his wedding day.

On this his wedding day a band of desperados rode into town, and all the men hid. Gary Cooper had to put on his badge and face the dangerous outlaws alone for the good of the people in town.

His wife gave him a hard time because she did not want him to perhaps be killed. But he had to fight them anyway. He didn't listen to his bride to be. He listened to his conscience instead.

There was a beautiful song, the theme of the move, sung by Frankie Laine: "Do not forsake me, oh my darling. For I must face the man who hates me or die a coward, a craven coward."

In this great movie, this noble hero fought the bad guys and won. Then he and his bride rode into the sunset to begin their life together. Had he been a coward, he would not have respected himself. And deep down, she would not have respected him either.

St. Augustine said it well. He said: "love God and do what thou wilst." In other words, love God (with all your heart mind and soul) and you can't do anything wrong or out of step.

Some persecuted Chinese Christians who were imprisoned for their Christian faith said it this way:

"Before prison we knew *about* God. After we were imprisoned, we *experienced* God."

Other thoughtful spiritual people have said the same thing. The Russian writer Alexander Solzhenitsyn, who was imprisoned for his truth speaking in a Siberian prison camp said: "thank God for prison."

Why is it that so many have found God in prison? It is because their imprisonment, especially the austere solitary confinement type, strips everything away. And when everything is gone, there is nothing left to interfere, to fill them with distraction. And so in sheer simplicity, the person discovers the still small voice.

Finally, Christ said it best: "Put first the Kingdom of God and His right way, and all other things will be added unto you." First check with intuition, first check with what you know in your heart, and make your moment by moment walk with God more important than anything else.

He also said: "the love of the world makes for enmity with God."

There is a state of awareness, a state of consciousness where one is closer to the inner source of intuition and guidance and a little distant from the world. The true Christian mystics down through the ages have tried to communicate this to us, but not very successfully. They found it for themselves, but are hard pressed to teach others how to find it.

Yet, many of us have tasted of it a little, though we probably didn't know what we were experiencing. For example, some of us have been in great danger; then for a moment we felt as if we were watching it happen to someone else, and during this observant state, the danger somehow passed and we were safe.

Others of us have suddenly had a strong intuition not to get in a car, get on an airplane or have anything to do with some person. Our intuition was warning us—protecting us from an accident or untoward incident.

Finally, some of us have suddenly felt a little distant when one of our loved ones was in grave condition at the hospital, for example. We experienced two things.

One, we suddenly realized (in the inner light of intuition) that all the trivial things we had been caught up in were unimportant. They paled in significance in comparison to the importance of our loved one.

Secondly, we may have felt a sense of calm composure come over us. We handled things, helped others, and kept our heads while others were upset. Yet, it was almost as if someone else were doing it. We were being guided by the Spirit.

Also, some of us just knew we had to pursue some line of interest or talent (even though others tried to dissuade us). Others of us had an idea for a business or an invention. It was truly creative and helped others.

This inspiration somehow came to us from within.

Or sometimes we just happened to be in the right place at the right time to meet our future wife, husband or benefactor; or someone mysteriously came into our life to help us just when we most needed it.

These were the help from God. We did not realize it, but we were being guided and protected.

Now, husbands and dads, take a deep breath, and sit in awe of what I have just said. Ask yourself--how close you are to this intuition of which I speak? Because it affords your family a protection.

Are you like George Washington who was observed in full military dress, on his knees in the snow praying, because nothing to him was more important than doing God's will? Or are you afraid of what your wife will say, what your kid's teacher will say, or what the boss will say? Do you cop out on principles because you want to be popular?

Are you perfectly honorable in every detail, in public and in private? Do you permit yourself no indulgence, such as too much socializing, silly talk, naughty jokes, or wrong food? Do you stand out like a sore thumb at times because your uprightness and honesty make others uncomfortable? Or are you a people pleaser?

Is your Creator Within the ground of your being, or is it your wife?

I don't need to go any further. All men have failed (the author included). Most men are women centered.

They love their wife more than God. They look to mom, wife, some floozy at the bar, or other womanly men to support them. Their wobbly egos especially seek sexual support to reassure them that animal man is the real man, and that sex is love.

We all inherit our fallen nature from our parents, and from their parents' parents all the way back to Adam and Eve. Adam lived in Paradise. Then he listened to his wife instead of God, and brought death upon himself and ushered in the jungle hell we see around us to this very today. Do you listen to intuition and abide by principle, or do you listen to your wife?

Adam was ambitious. He loved his own pride and some glorious future (career) more than he loved his wife or God. If he had really loved God, he would not have disobeyed Him. If he really loved his wife, he would have had the vision to see what his disobedience would bring upon her. But he was selfish. He set aside understanding (intuition) for pure knowledge (without understanding), because he believed that raw knowledge would make him successful.

When Adam fell, he began to change. Before his fall, he could have lived forever. But in separation from God through doubt and disobedience, death entered the human race.

Adam traded eternal life for a temporal life that leads to death. From regeneration through daily renewal and life from the Creator to live perpetually, he fell to have to procreate to make replacement bodies.

Thereby a sort of perpetuation would occur through making replacement bodies. That's the animal way, but it is nothing like the perpetual rejuvenation through closeness to God.

To this very day, we have modesty and inherited embarrassment over sexuality, because we all sense at some deep unplumbed level what it represents: the shame of our race's failing.

Before his fall, Adam's love life was being in-filled with life from the Creator. He could then share this love-life which came through him from God with his wife.

Today's modern Adam (unless he finds salvation) has temporal life to offer and sex love for perpetuation of the species. When he gives her his sex love, she drains him of energy from the storehouse of his life force, which he has only a limited amount of. The wife may become addicted to this life and demand it of him.

Should she become demanding and nagging, and he respond, he will give up his life that way. Now you know why men die first, and the woman goes on to often get cancer (when with her husband gone she has to start draining her own cells for the energy she had become dependent on from him).

What is missing in most relationships is the life and love from the Creator. In fact, it is true love. We call this love "agape love." It is emotionless. It is correcting.

A woman will give a man a hard time. She does not even know what it is that she wants from him, but the more she demands, the more he gives sex love or brings her flowers. And in lieu of the agape love she really needs, she will come to depend on and be addicted to the life force she can extract from him.

The positive love from God, which can come through a person but is not from the person, is a powerful force. It corrects, chastens, humbles, but also is tender and redeems, enlightens, warms, and sustains.

Husbands, do you now see why you must seek this love from God? It is good to be a decent husband, a good provider, and do the things a good husband and father does. But you also need to find a rapport with the Father. How and when this might happen I cannot say, other than it is a blessing. We must yearn for truth with all our heart, and we must cry out to God to give us answers and teach us what we need to know, and change us from our prideful ways.

Should the man find an inner bond with his Creator, he will love what is right more than anything, including his wife. But a good woman will not mind this at all. The man who loves principle more than anything is the man she can trust. He is the man who will not use her. He is the man that will never fail her. He is the man who will love her for herself, not as an object of use.

She will be able to let her hair down and just be her plain and simple uncorrected self. Just as all men have some Adam in them, all women have a little Eve in them. The noble husband will correct her guile and correct naughtiness. He will love her for herself, not for the hell in her. And through gently jousting with her spirit, he will draw forth the woman out of the female. Even as God draws forth the man out of the male.

She may test him to see if his new ways are for real. All she has ever known are weak men, so she may not believe he is different. Should she test him and find him not wanting, then she can feel secure. Both can live happily ever after.

- 14 -

Just How Important is Dad?

Many dads are decent and basically say the right things. Why then do their wives secretly resent them?

Why does the daughter feel he has failed her, and why is there a distance between her and him? Why is the son angry and rebellious?

And if the kids are conformists, seemingly doing all the right things, why do they go on to lives that end in disease and suffering? Why indeed.

The problem is that dad, although saying the right things, does not say them strongly enough. Most dads are wimps. They do the will of their wife and their boss.

They tow the party line, and they uphold the status quo.

Those dads who speak up strongly usually do so angrily; and the anger, being a failure, taints their message.

Other dads do honor what is right and do recognize what is right, but they stand silently by because of some feeling of inferiority or guilt. Such a dad fails to speak up because he does not feel qualified to do so. Or he fails to speak up because he is or was involved in the very thing he should speak up about.

In order to understand how dads fail and what the result is for their family, we will discuss the subject in detail.

From the outset, let me state the bottom line.

Dad stands in for God in the eyes of the child.

This is dad's role: he must represent what is right clearly and unmistakably. He cannot have any vices, and he must have outgrown or be in the process of outgrowing any need for worldly approval and support.

He must see clearly what is right and not doubt it. He must speak honestly and firmly about what is right without vacillation. He must also be able to express what is right without anger—anger itself being a failing.

The man of faith does not need anger to support himself or what he is saying. His invisible support comes from a bond with his Creator within.

He must also live what is right. He cannot lecture about drugs while holding a marijuana cigarette in his hand. Dad can only do these things if he has faith, wisdom, longsuffering, kindness, firmness, honor, and courage. Any doubt on his part, any vacillation, or any selfish indulgence, and he fails. And when he fails, the whole family suffers.

It is simply impossible for a dad to have the super strength and faith to withstand the subtle pressures of the world without an inner bond with his Creator. He must have the kind of relationship that Moses, David, the prophets, or Jesus had with the Father. If he looks to the church, to his wife, to his company, to medicine, to the doctor, to the government, or to anyone for support, his roots will go out into the world and he will fail.

That is why so called good Christians, who go to church and say all the right things, often ultimately fail and cause their families to secretly or openly suffer.

Their so called faith is emotional and is based on words, study, and other people's support. It is worldly in other words. All their churchianity saves them from is the Truth: that they have not yet found an inner bond with the Creator. They are Christian, but not Christian enough.

For the time being, let's put aside discussion of the violent, abusive, drunken, drug taking or womanizing man. He is obviously wrong and cannot possibly do any good. Let's also put aside discussion about the self righteous dad who forces religion on his family. He is also obviously wrong, and does far more harm than good.

Let's also put aside discussion of the hypocritical dad—who puts on an act for others but who is secretly wrong. He is also not credible and he gives religion and fatherhood a bad name.

About the above, I would say that there is not much hope for them unless they realize in the Light of Truth that they are wrong and become truly sorry and truly change.

Unfortunately, this is rare, because most people do not want to admit they are wrong. Even when they do, it is only to save their pride, put on a show for others, and prevent the loss of perks or privileges.

However, I will say that the dad who has a keen sense of justice and who is angry over injustice has a chance of recovering if he can see that it is anger and resentment that made him wrong. In other words, he is right about what he perceives and what he says. All he has to do is take the anger out of his message.

Let's talk about the average dad, who is basically decent. Him I can help. If he is angry, he must learn to give up anger; and he must learn to stand for what is right, not with anger, but with resolve and patient endurance.

The decent but wimpy dad must learn to give up the support of his wife, friends and other worldly affiliations. He must stand for what is right, instead of standing silently by with secret hostility and resentment.

He must stand up alone if necessary. He must only look to God for approval. But first he must search his heart and if he is still secretly resentful, he must first let go of the resentment. Otherwise, anything he says will be tainted with that resentment.

Before proceeding, let me say that as the child of a failing dad, your only hope of recovering from *your* problems is to forgive your parents, especially your dad.

Otherwise, your lack of forgiveness keeps you tied to his wrong, and makes you an extension of that wrong.

You will be destined to become like your dad or to continue hating and serving men like your dad all your life. As a lady, you will be compelled to keep finding men just like your dad, who you will judge and resent.

And this judgment will keep alive the wrong in you.

Your continuing unforgiveness will block you from recovery, and your continued emotionality will result in relationship, health, and financial problems.

Everyone thinks that mother is the most important person in the family, but it is actually dad. Even in his absence. Most kids today suffer from too much mom and not enough dad.

Father stands in for God in the eyes of the child.

When father fails, it is as if God had failed the child. At a very deep level, the child is wounded. Dads who are drunks, drug addicts, ambitious achievers, or womanizers are obviously wrong. But the importance of dad is such that even the half way decent dad--the one who goes to work every day and watches TV at

144

home every night—if he is not wise enough or strong enough to see the subtle dangers that seek to tempt his children to doubt truth and virtue will fail to protect his family and will allow them to be corrupted.

The weak but affable dad is likable enough. But being likable is not enough. Even saying the right things is not enough. The man must search for the strength, patience, wisdom, and virtue he cannot find in the world. He must look within, and he must not look to his wife to be his support.

Let's face it, all dads have failed their families. But wait! That is no excuse to resent him or hate him. If you resent your father, a wall is put up between you and the Creator. You remain tied to the error operating in your dad, and your unforgiveness blocks finding God's forgiveness.

Realize that perhaps you never really knew your real dad. What you saw was the error operating through him. And it got into him because he resented his failing parents.

Therefore, forgive your dad by dropping your grudges and judgments against him. You will then be free to find and express love from within. And you will be free to be a good mom or dad yourself.

- 15 -

Marriage Counseling for Men

"Men need to get a little clarification about what the husband's (dad's) really role is. For example, what your family really needs is for you to be strong and sure (without anger of course). "

"You need to be more like John Wayne and less like Mr. Rogers. More like Ronald Reagan and less like Jimmy Carter."

You need to pay more attention to what your family really needs from you than to what they say (or complain about). "

The truth is that sometimes we feel more comfortable with one person than another. And when it comes to counseling, many men would rather talk about their issues with another man.

The problem is that too much of what passes for counseling among men is really more like support, bonding, or guy talk.

If you need help with your golf swing, you need a good golf instructor. Maybe your friends or the guys in the club house will be fun to talk to. They may be supportive and understanding. They may even give you their two cents worth.

But what you really need is a first rate swing coach.

So when it comes to counseling, it's easy to find a sympathetic ear or support. But what you need is counseling that is more like what a good sports coach does.

In other words, you need someone who knows what they are talking about, can give you some really good tips, and send you on your way so you can start practicing doing the right thing the right way.

So let's say that you recognize that you need some help--with relationship issues, home/work balance, anger management, or whatever. What you are hoping for is a really good coach or mentor. You would like someone who has "been there, done that." Someone who is like a senior manager who can mentor you, offer some practical common sense advice, and then be there occasionally, if you need a little more feedback.

Perhaps most importantly, you want to hear it from an authority you can respect. Like a father, grandfather or successful senior mentor. You also don't want them to undermine your authority. It would also be nice if you could work one on one with the person--someone who wants to help you instead of seeing you as the problem. You would also like it to be one on one, not two or three against one.

Perhaps you decide to turn to the clergy--a minister or a chaplain. This is good because the pastor or chaplain will hopefully see you as a person, a whole person with mind, body and soul--and treat you like a whole person.

But too often, what you get is a sympathetic listener, nice platitudes, something to study, and supportiveness.

They tell you to be nice, put little love notes on the refrigerator, wash the dishes and help your wife vacuum.

Someone once said that being nice means being weak.

We like nice people. Nice people are easy to be around. Nice people make you feel comfortable. But nice people will not confront you with the plain truth.

They soften their words so as not to offend, thus rendering themselves ineffective.

Nevertheless, there is a natural tendency to think that when things are going wrong with our relationships (with our partner, our kids, or at work) that learning to be nice is the answer.

I have to say, and I say this with love because I am a pastor myself, too much of what passes for pastoral counseling, Christian counseling, or what we hear in church is about being "nice."

Please don't ask whether I'm saying that we should be mean and angry. Of course not.

But I know too many men who are nice--they go to work every day, they are home every evening, they are a nice guy--and their family walks all over them. Mom is in charge, and she resents him for his weakness.

Of course, many men go to the opposite extreme in order to try to restore order, and they become angry and mean. But this is clearly wrong. Anger and meanness are failings. When you are weak and wimpy, your family will not respect you. When you are angry, your family will hate you and will not respect you either.

Until you learn the secret of self control, the only choices you have are the extremes--anger and violence or resentful weak submission.

What many men end up doing is becoming resentfully repressed. They get all bottled up and say nothing, but underneath they are full of secret hostility and resentment. High blood pressure or ulcers anyone?

There has to be an answer. And there is. It's like avoiding the extremes, but not quite. It's more like firm but fair. It means loving justice and what is right and standing for what is right, but with a twinkle in your eye. A man needs patience, kindness, tender heartedness, long suffering, and gentleness. But he also needs to STAND FOR SOMETHING.

Therefore, if you have always been Mr. Nice guy and have found that it doesn't work, but you don't want to be Mr. Meany either--then you need a little basic training about how to stand for what is right without anger. And about why virtue gets respect.

I have been advising and counseling people for over 20 years. I have to say that most people who come to me for help are women. Women are keener to detect something going wrong in a relationship, for example.

Men tend to not sense something is wrong until it gets really critical and she demands a divorce or something.

I think women suffer more in relationships than men do. They are more aware in relationships than men are.

I'm focusing on relationships because they are so important. What makes our personal failings so painful is that they always involve others. As dad and father, you are supposed to be the Moses, the George Washington of your family. Your family looks to you for guidance, strength, kindness and understanding.

When you are wimpy, you fail them. When you are angry, you fail them. When you are not there for them, you fail them.

I have some understanding in this area. I can help you because even though I am a man, I have some insight into what your wife or kids are most likely feeling. They may not be able to tell you what they feel--but I can.

Okay, it may be tough love. But remember--for your golf swing, you want a good swing coach. In a counselor, you need someone who will tell you the truth with love.

If a teenager completes a task—he appreciates an honest assessment. He doesn't want someone to criticize and put him down, but he also doesn't want someone to condescendingly tell him how "wonderful" something is (when he knows it isn't). He wants an honest assessment and feedback so that he can improve his performance. From a counselor, you need someone who knows what he is talking about and who can give you some honest feedback and real solutions.

- *16* -

Men, Straighten Up and Fly Right

Some wives are so possessive of their husband's loyalty that they will secretly resent and fear a man's inner bond with his Creator.

A man must have a devil-may care-attitude toward what others think of him. If he sees a right course to steer, then he must be like Noah, Moses or Columbus-- inwardly inspired and doing what he needs to do regardless of what others think or say.

Don't look for emotional support from your wife. A wife can be a tremendous helpmate. But if you look to your wife for support of who you are or what you do, you are casting her into the role of God, and the temptation in her will rise up to enslave you and rule you.

Frankly, it's almost better to have a wife that tries to cast doubt on every move you make, because that way, through your suffering (and seeing her agony) you will learn to be a man and look within for support.

The man whose wife is very supportive of everything he does very often finds her in charge of his life. Not only does he become dependent on her support, but he will also resent her when he discovers she feels it her right to delve into every aspect of his life. Ladies tend to be a bit possessive and think that they own their guy.

Don't resent her for this. Love your wife, and do what you see is right not because she tells you to or lets you, but because you see that it is right.

A wife may also become a grace robber of even technically proper actions. For example, many a man has turned over the religious upbringing of the children to the wife. If he really had a bond with internal intuition, he would see that it is his responsibility as husband to oversee the very delicate care and protection of his children's souls.

Most men wash their hands of the child's education, turning his authority over to the wife, the external church, the school system, and so-called experts and bureaucrats. Even if his wife is doing a good job of attending to the education of the kids—if dad is not involved, something is wrong. Though technically things are proceeding along okay, her being in charge has usurped her husband's duty, and kids will sometimes rebel from school or church, because they detect dad's default.

It is better if dad stays in charge of the kid's education and church activities. If he has to delegate responsibility to wife or others, it will be okay if he remains watchful and involved.

For the type of men who becomes addicted to a woman's support, you will observe that bosses, bartenders, the other woman, or his support group are just substitutes for the nagging wife he gave power to and then ran from. Many men become little more than yes-men, rubber stamping whatever their wives, doctors, teachers or bureaucrats decide.

Some of the children of the characterless father who leans on his wife for support will grow up to be characterless conformists, stooges and shills for the worldly system and addicted to its perks, just as he was.

Some of the children, especially the more perceptive ones, will rebel against the nagging authority of mom or the arbitrary, condescending, or even wicked authority of strangers.

Such children look bad--though most of their acting-out is actually a cry for true love which should come from the father. Mom cannot really be blamed either, because she's simply stepping up to fill the vacuum caused by dad's absence or abdication.

Some women are power hungry and love the power they get. But decent women are troubled by the responsibility handed over to them. They wish their husband would step up and take his proper fatherly role, but most of the time he is more like a big kid himself.

I'm not blaming moms. Dad is responsible. If the suffering of his wife and children does not waken him to see his need for understanding, wisdom and courage, then nothing will. Blaming his wife is just another cop out for his own failing. It's another way his ego finds to make itself look blameless.

Many women are single moms nowadays. She has no choice but to do the best she can without a husband there. The first thing she must do is learn to not resent and judge her former husband, boyfriend, her dad, or men in general. The men failed her; but through understanding gained from meditating, she will come to see that all men are failures. A few will wake up; most won't. Their weakness tempts her to play the role of his ground of being and then resent him when he falls for her temptation. She must see that this no-win game is a trap.

As Ann Landers said: "It takes two to tango. It also takes two to tangle." The decent woman must awaken to see her own role in failing relationships. When she does, her dropping of resentment and judgment will open up her own heart to receive grace and inner love from her Creator within.

Though some men are cads, many men are decent.

They might even one day find themselves and grow to be very noble. But the hard time that many wives give their husbands keeps them resentful and fixated to pleasing or appeasing her. In this type of resentment-based pressure cooker of suppressed emotions, he may not have enough space to find himself.

In most marriages, both remain asleep, fixated to each other through resentment, blame, and guilt.

In some marriages, one person wakes up and stops playing games. Sometimes the new found awareness of the one will help the other wake up. If this happens then both partners will bring into being a heaven on earth. If only one wakes up, that person must suffer in dignity.

At least that person will stop supporting the wrong in the other and can stop feeling guilty for that.

If you, as a man, are beginning to wake up, here is a little advice. First, bear the pain of seeing your own failing and wrong in quiet dignity. Mourn in private, but go out into the world with a cheerful countenance.

Your wife, who you have been abusing through anger (which makes her in charge of your beastly self) or through wimpiness, will undoubtedly not believe your new found grace.

Don't ask for her forgiveness (which again puts her in the God role). Make a brief, sincere but unemotional apology for your past failing to be the man you should be, and then say "from now on things will be different."

Go about your business. Don't try to make up for past errors; just live properly from now on.

Chances are she will test you for a long time to see if you are sincere. This will be your chance to practice longsuffering, forbearance, patience, and wisdom.

Above all, before you begin seeking to correct others, make sure that you, yourself, are coming from a good place. Obtain a copy of the free meditation we offer and practice it to help you be calm and reasonable.

I know that many of you who are starting to wake up face very difficult circumstances you have brought on yourselves. Divorces, rebellious children, health problems, and financial problems can sometimes appear almost impossible to solve.

It may seem hopeless at times. But take heart. "With God all things are possible." Just remember to put first things first. Meditate for objectivity. Then through objectivity will come understanding and patience. Do not seek to roll up your sleeves and try to solve your problems egotistically.

That's what you have always done, and it hasn't worked. Now you must learn faith. Stand back and observe your symptoms and circumstances without resentment or upset. Realize your role in their creation.

Suffer in dignity the pain of seeing the mess you have helped make. Wait to be repented. Let go and let God.

If you do not look to anyone or anything else to relieve your suffering, God will lift your burden. In due course, He will straighten out your life.

Given time, some of your loved ones might even come around. In the meantime, do what you can, realizing that you do not deserve grace. Be grateful to be given the power to stand back and observe your wrongs, and be grateful for a second chance to make things right.

- 17 -

Are There No More Good Men Left

Yes, there are. Unfortunately, many of them are misguided about what it means to be a man. The media would have you believe that men are dumb, uncool, beer drinking sports junkies, or at best crass shallow ambitious types.

When men buy into this degrading view of themselves, it works to the advantage of the advertisers and those who want power over them.

That's why they tempt the man into acting like a party animal or sports junkie where little is expected of him.

But if he falls for the ruse and buys into this type of behavior, his wife and other people won't have any respect for him. He will also find that he has no authority in his home and is generally treated with contempt.

On the other hand, some men are angry and violent.

They are obviously wrong. Their anger may frighten some people, but these men are of weak character.

They are easily tempted to anger. And because of their anger, they are not only wrong, but also get in trouble. Watch out for anger—it is a failing.

But how about all the decent men who go to work, earn a living, and spend their weekends with their family or working in the yard? Unfortunately, these decent men are often also held in contempt by the media and by those who basically don't like men.

How is that otherwise good and decent men are so self conscious, self doubting, and generally feel like they need advice about how to communicate or be men? It is because they have become outer directed and subject to the very ones who hold them in contempt.

Today power goes to the institutions and a sea of experts, writers, pundits, counselors, educators, social workers, ministers, and facilitators. A long time ago it was: "Father Knows Best." Now it is: everyone knows best except father. That's how the so-called helpers get power and make a good living off of your weakness and failing.

The key to restoring order, harmony, love and understanding in the marriage relationship has to do with waking up and seeing the truth.

For every home where there is a violent father, mother, or guardian, there are many homes where everyone is decent but are held in subtle contempt by other members of the family who have bought the lie.

The media and the advertisers appeal to the lowest common denominator. Most people are far, far more human and sophisticated than they are portrayed as.

Dad may not be dumb or uncommunicative. He may be quiet because he is kind or knows that his words would be misinterpreted.

He may live a simple old-fashioned life, not because he is unsophisticated, but because he is giving up many selfish pursuits and excitements for the good of the family.

I know of a sad story where a college counselor convinced a wife to divorce her husband, who was regarded as decent but dumb, so she could "do her own thing." The kids, closer to her and viewing themselves as educationally superior to their behind-the-times dad, took her side. Soon the whole family was in rebellion against dad.

Bear in mind that he was decent, hard working, non drinking, nonviolent, and not womanizing. The divorce destroyed the family, hurt the kids and ruined both of their finances. Sadly she got lupus and then cancer. He died alone. Years later, the kids realized that dad wasn't as bad as they had thought. But it was too late.

Meanwhile the college counselor who talked her into divorcing did not have to even suffer any inconvenience for her social experimentation.

Yes, some men are no good. And, yes, some women are no good. Just make sure that something, such as the entertainment media, has not gotten between you and your beloved spouse or between you and your beloved kids--and fed your mind with false notions and suggestions instead of human understanding.

Marriage is a union and a bond, both physical and psychic. Believe it or not, marriage is sacred.

Admittedly, most people marry for the wrong reasons; but marriage is a wonderful opportunity to learn not to be selfish.

And I have to say: what goes wrong with the family is the father's fault. He holds a very special office: the office of fatherhood. The man must wake up to see that he is not being a man. He cannot be violent, and he cannot be a wimp. He must have the patience of Job and the wisdom of Solomon. He must not fail.

The media and others who want his power will never stop tempting him and seeking to degrade him. He must see what is going on and simply stay the course.

A husband and father must be principled, honorable, patient, wise, longsuffering, and kind. He must have the courage of conviction. He must make principle more important than anything. He has to be able to stand on his own feet, know what is right, and do what is right-- without his wife's or anyone else's support.

When the man sobers up and realizes what is required of him, he will throw away his drink, drugs, and marijuana. Sports and entertainment will return to their proper place--rest and recreation after a life well led. He will do what is right even if it means not being popular.

He will stand for what is right, with courage and kindness; and will not need the support of a wife, friends, peers, support group, or church. He will reach within and find an invisible means of support: and his aloneness and honor will breed respect.

The good men are there, but they must step up to the plate. Husbands--your wife and your children need you to be the noble knight in shining armor. If you will, Sir, be that man.

- *18* -

Can I Reconcile with My Husband, Wife, or Child?

The short answer is yes. The somewhat longer answer: Yes, but. . . . . .

There are many factors involved, as well as complications. The other person may not want to.

Especially if you were not a very good husband, wife, or parent.

Perhaps things were going south, but you were too busy or a little naive. You didn't see what was happening until a crisis hit--such as she filed for divorce, he found someone else, or a child ran away from home.

Maybe, for example, you weren't a very good husband, wife or parent. You were angry, resentful, and selfish. You were only thinking about yourself and became resentful when your needs weren't met.

Perhaps now you see what your error was. You are sorry and have really and truly changed. But too much water has gone under the bridge. Your ex has remarried, or your adult child hates you and refuses to return your call.

If your change of heart is phony--just another way of trying to save your ego, get back a former cushy way of life, or if it is just to get rid of guilt by trying to get them to tell you that everything is now okay--it won't work.

But as I said, suppose you really and truly have changed. You have grown up and matured. You have given up your resentments and are sorry for your former selfishness. You've thrown away your drugs, marijuana, or booze.

If you were a criminal, you are now clean: you have paid your debt to society, and have never, never gone back to old associations or activities for years. You've reset your priorities and no longer make sex, money, career or whatever you misused for ego purposes too important. Now you are ready to be a good father, a loving wife, or a patient parent.

But if the other person has gone away and does not want to talk to you, then you must leave them alone.

Sure, if you are really and truly sorry for your part in what went wrong, you can write a letter. But that's about all. Move on and live the good life. Hold your head up high.

Another scenario. The two of you have had issues, maybe a separation, but you are in the process of cleaning up your act and the other person is still open to the idea of reconciliation—in this situation there is hope. If there has been a divorce, but both of you remain unmarried, that makes getting back together possible.

Bear in mind that t*he key to a new lease on life hinges on your reconciliation with conscience.*

If you reconcile with conscience (what you know in your heart is right), that makes the possibility of other good things happening possible. Remember what Christ said: "Put first the Kingdom of God and His right way, and all other things will be added unto you."

Therefore--first things first. Put aside fixating on the other person, either with blame or with resentful longings over what you've lost out on. Instead focus on cleaning up your own act and getting right with God.

Just remember, it has to be real, not phony.

Take heart in these words of the Messiah: "With man it would be impossible, but with God, all things are possible."

Just live the good life. It may not be possible to reconcile. Sometimes, even if you have changed, the other person may not have. Or they refuse to forgive. If so, then just let them go.

Live your life in dignity. If you should remarry, then be the good husband or wife. Just be a decent person.

Watch out for the trap of trying too hard to make things work in your new marriage.

Maybe years from now, your kids from your former marriage will want to re-establish contact with you. If so, be prepared to listen to what they have to say about what you did to them. You may have forgotten, but they have not. Acknowledge the truth.

I believe that the family is the foundation of society. I would like to see people living happily ever after.

I believe that those who are living together and who have a real marriage of the heart, will one day, with grace, perhaps come to formalize their togetherness.

I believe that those who are divorced, but who have never remarried, may one day think back on their youthful selfishness and wish they could come back together again. For some, it will be possible. For others, simply deeply and truly forgiving the other person will be liberating, and will even psychically free the other person, though a thousand miles away.

I believe that those who have remarried (if they don't try too hard to make the second or third marriage work and end up copping out on principle for peace) will be able to work out their issues this time and become a better spouse and father, if they can learn to forgive and to be unselfish.

I believe that if the children of troubled marriages can find a way not to resent their parents, they can be free to become happy and balanced adults, and one day spouses and parents, without having to bring the baggage of the past into the future.

I believe that kids who are now or who have resented their parents can, with a little understanding, come to forgive their parents. And if they do, and if they learn to be friends with their conscience, they will recover from the trauma of having resented their parents. They will be able to leave the sad legacy of dysfunctionality behind, and be free to become good parents themselves.

- 19 -

How Do I Become More Forgiving?

It's hard to express faith and patience when we are upset. It's hard to be forgiving when we are angry. It is hard to express love when we are resentful. Therefore, I have come to the inescapable conclusion that if we could learn to remain calm in the moment of stress instead of upset and resentful--we can be better people.

This is especially of importance to Christians who know they are supposed to be forgiving, but don't know how. Resentment (and its handmaidens judgment, anger, and upset) block love and patience.

Learn to let go of resentment, and you will discover that it is the same as being forgiving. Forgive by not hating. Forgive by not resenting. Forgive by not judging.

You don't have to do something—such as like the other person, for example. Just don't resent them. That's all.

Another thing, we all know that we are supposed to be reasonable, forgiving and patient. But it is hard to do so when under pressure. For example, the Christian learns wonderful Biblical principles in church, Sunday school, or listening to Christian radio, but when under stress, we become upset, angry, or impatient.

We say the wrong thing or feel the wrong thing (resentment). Then we escape into thinking where we try to rearrange the past, excuse our failing, or worry and scheme about the future.

When we keep failing to apply the principles that we love, we become frustrated and angry at ourselves. But all this does is add another layer of upset.

The answer is to learn how to respond properly to stress, instead of reacting and becoming upset. Actually the proper response is not to respond emotionally at all, but to remain impassive (through responding to inner wisdom and principle).

At the Center for Common Sense Counseling, we teach the "how" of remaining patient and more forgiving. By learning the simple technique of how to remain centered and calm, we are pre-armed with Godly grace. It is anger and upset that wash away patience and reason. In other words, we can learn how to hang onto our patience by not becoming upset. We can hang onto a forgiving attitude by not letting stress sneak up on us and render us judgmental.

It is spiritual discipline that we need. But not the type that comes from suppressing anger or putting on a good face with seething resentment underneath. It is the discipline of learning how to get centered and then from that calm center of dignity clearly seeing our need for patience.

When the stressful situation arrives (often involving a delicate moment with our spouse, parent, or child), we meet the moment with grace, instead of reacting with the usual upset and coming unglued.

In simple terms, if we could learn the secret of not getting upset, we can be better Christians.

The Center for Common Sense Counseling is a nondenominational outreach to all people. I have no organization to join or belong to. My mission is to awaken people to their conscience and to what they know in our hearts, and then I wish to offer a few tips on how to stay in touch with that good by not becoming upset or resentful.

"My brethren, count it all joy when ye fall into divers temptations; Knowing this, that the trying of your faith worketh patience.

But let patience have her perfect work, that ye may be perfect and entire, wanting nothing." James 1: 2-4

- *20* -

Is Food Your Secret Lover and Enabler?

Food offers a mysterious salvation and escape for us humans. And because it offers escape and comfort, we turn to it when our ego is hurting, when we need our anger soothed, or our anxiety taken away.

For each of us, food has both a personal history and one that is inherited along with our heritage as a human.

When life is boring, we look for something distracting or exciting. When life is boring we look for something to excite our imagination.

When life makes us uneasy and nervous or anxious, or when we have a hard time coping with what we see, we look for escape.

Our salvation comes by way of the two-fer we get from food. It offers both a pleasurable escape, as well as comfort.

The comfort part is easy to understand. Food fills our tummy and takes away hunger. It also is associated with childhood memories of mother, her love, and her food.

So when our ego needs comfort, it turns to the mother love that food represents.

The escape aspect has both a natural and a supernatural aspect to it. The down to earth part is the simple fact that food offers a pleasurable diversion when, for example, we eat a nice meal, have a snack, or enjoy a sandwich with the Internet, newspaper, or television. In short, it is a pleasant break to eat.

But in a more profound sense, food also has a hypnotic quality. It ushers in dream time. We float away with our favorite food, and we are carried away from reality. Watch people sometime in a restaurant. As soon as they start eating, they are gone--off to a very private munching world.

We celebrate with food, but we also escape with food. When our life is not going well, when we have issues and problems, when we don't feel good about ourselves, when people are upsetting us--we turn to food for comfort and escape.

When we are unwilling to face some truth, or we are anxious and guilty over the way we are behaving or treating others—we use the hypnotic escape trigger of food to deny truth and escape conscience. We may only vaguely sense at some unplumbed depth that we are really avoiding God and His truth.

Food seems to understand us--just as a mother might—comforting, forgiving, and reassuring us that everything is alright. Just as sleep is an escape for some people, so is the food trance.

Here is another very important aspect of why we have such a relationship with food. Food fills the emptiness.

When we feel empty and unloved, many of us turn to food to love us and fill the void. That's why many of us have food problems.

A young lady whose dad is not there for her might find a sort of substitute love in food.

A married woman, whose husband is not there for her (or who she resents), may find "love" in food.

A man, who was close to his mom, might now be his own chef and cook for himself (thereby loving himself).

Of course, it is a small stretch to see how marijuana comforts and reassures certain people; or how another person will turn to alcohol (a variation of food) to comfort himself. Cigarettes, coffee, soda or even sipping on bottled water all day offer an oral comfort reminiscent of our early food gratification and assurance. The heroin addict even finds a sort of love in heroin, as it carries him away to his drug induced fog.

Here is a key principle to bear in mind: the human being is created in the image of God. Our soul should be loved and reassured by its Creator. But most of us do not have a bond with our Creator within. Most of us have not really found Him (though some will, and that is what I am trying to help you to do). Something gets in the way of being close to our Creator and having His love.

Did you accept your mother's love (food) and reject your dad? Was sit your will to reject your father, or her will? Can you see how archetypal this is? It is symbolic of accepting worldly love and rejecting father and the God that father is supposed to represent.

Love is a transforming thing. Who loves you also shapes what you become. Now you are undoubtedly not in the image of your Creator, but reshaped in the image of your mother, your violent or wimpy dad or some other worldly types.

If you were to find an inner rapport with God, then you would not need the love of the world. You could be a good wife, husband, or neighbor, enjoying fellowship with others--but you would not need other's love. If you found the life of the spirit that would come from within, you would not need distractions, diversions, or escapes. You would enjoy reality. You would live and move and have your being in the light and love of the Creator. Life would be exciting in a quiet way, and you would receive an invisible comfort from being in the good graces of God.

You would still find a modest pleasure in food, friends, work, exercise and so on. But nothing would become too important. You could be moderate in all your ways. You could eat to live instead of live to eat (or drink or party).

We are separated from God by pride. We do not want to become still before the inner light of conscience and admit we are wrong. And because we are avoiding conscience, we can receive no comfort from conscience. Instead we have to keep running from reality into the comforting arms of whoever or whatever helps us escape from conscience.

We are also separated from the love of God through resenting and judging others. We resent our mom, dad, husband, wife, or neighbor. We judge people for their errors and imperfections. And we harbor grudges against them. This resentment of others separates us from the love of God. It says in the Bible: "You cannot hate your brother who you can see and love the Father you cannot see."

Next time you become angry and resentful--notice how you become hungrier and thirstier. Resentment and wrong living excite and awaken a lust for life. But the piper has to be paid—we become enslaved by whatever we use to improperly comfort ourselves. We lose the approval of God and we become dependent on our worldly comforters to soothe our pain.

A wife can have food problems because she resents and judges her husband.

God is ever ready to love and help us, but we fend Him off by running from what we wordlessly know in our heart is right. And He also will not forgive us unless we first forgive others.

So we become locked in a love-hate relationship with people, objects and substances. We resent them, and then we love (need) them for the distraction or comfort value they provide. But when we accept their comfort, we then hate them for what they do to us.

This love-hate aspect is also seen in such things as binge eating. For example, food may represent mother and her will. And her will, which we once resented and struggled against, now is embodied in the food which we now struggle with. Food also represents false love.

Beneath mother's catering and food service there may have been a resentment of her husband, perhaps even of the kids. Eating her food meant accepting her will and partaking of her judgment and resentment. Often she draws an invisible unspoken line in the sand: eat my food and reject your father, or suffer my rejection and wrath.

Years later, the adult child struggles with food, having the same relationship with that food that she once had with mother.

So, now perhaps you can see why struggle is not the answer. Understanding is the answer. If you will, visit my website and blogs to read more about the food mystery that has the whole human race in its grasp. If you receive the message I offer with the right spirit, it might mark the beginning of a gradual return to a right relationship with food by way of a right relationship with God.

172

- *21* -

Pastor Roland Talks to Husbands and Dads

I have said many times that what goes wrong in the family is dad's fault. It is a man's job to be the father and head of household. He holds a very special office: the office of fatherhood.

Father stands in for God in the eyes of a child. The man must not fail. It is his duty, his obligation, and his mandate to do his duty, regardless of what difficulties come his way. He is like a good and noble sea captain.

He must do his duty, no matter what.

Thus father must be steadfast, principled, honorable, kind, patient, longsuffering, and he must have the courage of conviction to do what is right regardless of what others think.

When things get a little rough, dad is like the airline captain of a plane experiencing turbulence. The pilot remains calm, regardless of how others might be over-reacting.

People look to him for guidance and security. He does not let them down. Dad must be the same way.

He does not take counsel of his fears. He never waivers. He stays the course. And when the trouble is over—everyone is glad that he remained calm.

Because he represents God and stands for good, he must not have any vices. Whatever weaknesses or areas of some immaturity he might still have, he is in the process of outgrowing them.

The failing man must wake up, realize his wrong, see the need for him to be there for the family, and he must begin to fail less. And even as he still fails (though less and less), his new awareness and grace will mitigate the effects.

He stands for what is right. He is not there to win a popularity content. He does not look for support from others. He has an internal bond with conscience. He does not reach out and look for support; he reaches within for wisdom and courage.

All men have failed (with one exception, Jesus, Who never failed), going all the way back to Adam.

In the Garden of Eden, all Adam had to do, when his wife tempted him, was to say: "No, Dear. Father says we are not supposed to eat of that tree."

But the serpent (who was the most subtle of creatures) was very clever. Instead of approaching Adam directly, he operated through Eve. She spoke the doubt and ambitious words that he (the serpent) coached her to say.

Nevertheless, if Adam had really loved God, he would not have disobeyed God. And if he really loved Eve, he would have realized what his disobedience would bring upon her. But the temptation found a weakness in Adam. He was tempted to pride through his response to the suggestion. He was excited by the suggestion. And the emotions he felt in the presence of temptation separated him from faith through doubt and emotion. He becomes ambitiously excited to try making it on his own.

To this very day, men feel excitement in the presence of women, especially naughty ones.

You know the rest of the story. He reached for the fruit of knowledge (don't today's modern serpents say that education is the key to success)? And in so doing, he brought death on the whole human race. He failed in other words, and his failure made life miserable for his wife and for his progeny.

Ever since, all men have been failures. Each in his own way recreates the scene in the Garden. He turns his back on principle in order to take advantage of a young lady. Or he forgets principle and takes drugs to get a high and feel like God. He is tempted to lord it over others with money, power, street smarts, or intellectual knowledge. Or he is tempted to try to solve humanity's problems through technology without God. Some are even tempted by religious knowledge, as if having Bible knowledge would make us holy or good.

Because we men are all born in the lineage of Adam and Eve, we are born with egos that need support and reassurance. We look to our mothers to support and reassure us. Later we go out into the world and look for a woman to tempt and excite us, and to make us feel like a god. But when we fall and use her to support our ego, we then become subject to her.

Each new generation is born into the home with an unloved uncorrected woman and a weak wimpy or weak violent man as dad.

Most men are just like big kids themselves, looking to wife-momma to soothe their wounded pride and reassure them.

He looks to her (instead of God) for validation, assurance, motivation, and comfort. Thus she becomes his god. He turns his back on the real God, and makes her his temptation god. When she becomes too witchy or demanding, or when she does not provide enough exciting temptation for him, he looks to other women, other men, alcohol, drugs, money, or female imprinted bosses to play the role of tempter.

Thus his ground of being is in the woman, and beyond her in temptation and the source of temptation.

Instead of giving love, he demands love for his ego.

Pity the poor wife. She married him in the hope that he might become the knight in shining armor who would rescue her from her own dark side. She was aware of his weaknesses, but she hoped that her love would cure him and that she could change him.

She had a dad who was not there for her. She went out in the world looking for love. What she got was use and abuse.

If she is a decent woman, she hoped that she could capture him with her charms, but that he would then become more fatherly and provide the mysterious love she had never known.

What she really needs is to be corrected from her role as Eve temptress. Once ensconced in the marriage and with kids, he needs to wake up (perhaps by seeing her suffering), and to gradually become more mature and less selfish. He has to wake up to see what his family's real needs are.

Through him, because of his commitment to principle within, would come agape, emotionless love.

This love—kind, patient, calm, reasonable, and strong—would gently correct her of the need to play the role of temptress. She would be able to let her down and just be herself, secure that he would be there for her.

She would try him to test his mettle, perhaps for years. His steadfastness, his aloneness, his loyalty, and his kind strength would earn her respect, and one day perhaps her love. She could happily give herself to this noble man and come into his heavenly world, leaving her hell behind. Then they would live happily ever after.

What usually happens, however, is that she starts to become angry and unhappy. Her love, instead of making him into a prince, makes him more selfish.

Remember--she has a memory of use and abuse from men (including her father for not being there for her). She has an imprinted memory of weak or weak and violent men failing her and being users. She spots weakness a mile away, and it tempts her to judge.

Men's weakness and failing tempts her to puff up in contempt. When she feels guilty for her judgment, she serves him out of guilt. But her service only makes him weaker and more wrong.

And so around and around they go, both feeding each other's wrong, and both reinforcing their judgment of each other.

Gentlemen, your wife undoubtedly had a father who wasn't there for her, and she may have been used by other men. Then when you fail her or use her to support your ego, it awakens the memory of the trauma and reinforces her judgment.

Your failing tempts her to puff up in judgment. She feels a hate, but it is a superior hate for the dog husband who begs for her support and then takes advantage. Her contempt breeds disrespect. Can you see how your failing tempts her to become more angry and contemptuous?

In fact, even if you became the noble knight and tried to do the right thing, and were not using her—a woman who has been abused may still interpret your touch as abuse, or your kindness as weakness. Remember, she and all the other Eves since the beginning, have only known failing men.

It is said that a cat, having once sat on a hot stove, will never again sit on *any* stove. Your resentful wife just might interpret everything you do as use or failing, because you are a man, who she judges to be like all other men.

Now do you see why you must never fail? And since you have failed, now you must wake up, do some soul searching, and become committed to what is right, learning to fail less and eventually never.

Can you see why you need superb patience, super human strength of character, the patience of Job and the wisdom of Solomon? You need the understanding and agape love that you do not yet have. So you must seek within, crying out to your Creator, to give you what you don't deserve, and help you to have the wisdom to deal with your spouse and children with kindness, courage, and love.

I'm sorry to say that most men are rather dumb when it comes to relationships. Most men seem to think that all it takes is being nice or bringing flowers. When their wife becomes unhappy and claims that he is not communicating, he brings even more flowers.

He keeps trying harder and harder, perhaps even going to counselors and seminars where he learns to talk more, reveal all his weaknesses, give foot massages and put love notes on the refrigerator.

Eventually, he might become a total wimp, worshipping his wife and walking around on egg shells.

He does not know what she really needs. And while we are on the subject—though she is more aware than he is about what is going on, she probably does not know what she really needs either. And neither do all the misguided marriage counselors, therapists, marriage ministers, and relationship experts whose own lives are a mess.

But what she does know BIG TIME is that she is *not* getting it.

Men simply cannot understand why the unhappier she becomes, and the more he tries being nicer and more lovey dovey, the more unhappy or disturbed she becomes.

I am going to keep it all very simple. At first it may not seem like what I am saying is right, but all you have to do is look at the marriages and relationships you have known to see that something is going on that befuddles the participants and the so called experts too.

Despite six thousand years of human history and today's glut of experts, counselors, internet sites, books, and college courses by the tens of thousands--men and women still squabble, fight and become miserable.

Marriages break up or go on with seething resentment and unhappiness underneath. Meanwhile, the kids suffer. Somehow we are individually and collectively missing the boat.

So if you are serious about wanting to be a better husband or dad, then read on.

Humans are not apes or kangaroos. People have a soul. There is a spiritual dimension to life. And there are rules that govern our soul. Without an understanding of what has gone wrong, we will keep making the same mistakes. So it is evident that you must be ready to think outside the box. Sit back, relax, and I'll tell you a story. And maybe, as I tell the story, your eyes will be opened, and you will be able to see how it applies to the relationship between your parents and to your own current situation.

I will never forget something I read in a psychology book, where they were talking about imprinting. A young bird was studied to see if it would react to shadow images moving across the ceiling. No shape was responded to—until a silhouette moved across the ceiling that resembled the shape of a hawk. The little bird became agitated and attempted to run for cover.

Every member of this species reacted the same way, even though these particular birds had never before seen a hawk. It is a genetic or species memory.

In the trauma scene, when a sudden shock occurs, the animal (or human) is imprinted by everything in the scene. Everything in the scene forms a memory, and later when any element of the original trauma scene is reintroduced, the body reacts as if the whole scene were being repeated.

So there is trauma to an individual; and there is also a species trauma. It is the nature of the little bird to react to anything that resembles a circling hawk. The trauma leads to a memory. An individual memory or, in the case of the bird, a species wide memory.

It is said that a cat that sits on a hot stove will never sit on any stove. It will forevermore make that cat avoid any stove. I suppose that if the trauma were deep enough, penetrating right down to the very spiritual identity of the cat, it might result in little cats being born who were by nature wary of stoves.

Now let's look at humans. Could it be that the trauma in the Garden of Eden involving knowledge, food, the woman and deceitful words could have been so deep and profound that it forevermore altered the human race? I think so.

The proof is all around you. You see men reacting with a psycho-spiritual excitement to the presence of a woman (because of what she represents to the male's ego). This response is almost genetic.

You see women motivating and then resenting their weak ambitious men. You see the whole human race affected by food and having food problems. And everywhere you see people worshipping at the tree of education, with lying deceitful politicians ruling the fallen masses.

In light of what I have just said, let's look at what happened in the Garden of Eden. When Adam ate of the fruit, it was a big trauma. Suddenly, he lost the approval of his Father, he lost Paradise, and his whole life was suddenly ruined.

In the moment of shock, his eyes were opened in an animal way. He saw Eve differently than before.

Before he was innocent and he did not know sin. His consciousness changed. Some of you have felt this change after having taken drugs for the first time or engaged in a first promiscuous activity. Afterwards, in one way you felt you had grown (in a worldly way). But something was lost. Your friends slapped you on the back for being initiated into a lower realm of knowing, but deep down you sensed that you had lost some sweetness you had before.

Adam became imprinted with the image of the woman. Just as the little bird senses danger when a silhouette resembling a hawk circles, the image of the woman is indelibly imprinted in the psyche of all men.

She represents excitement, party time, ambition, and danger.

And through their mothers, men also see the woman as comfort to soothe and reassure their wounded pride.

For Eve, the trauma also brought a knowledge of failing. She became imprinted with the image of the man. The man represents failing and loss.

When a lady is little, father represents good and security. She hopes to one day meet a man who is good like the idealized father and live happily ever after. But somehow the interaction with men—her earthly failing father, and later boyfriends and husband—awakens her to men's failing, and this failing reminds her of the mysterious fall, etched deep in her psyche, where men first failed woman and Paradise was lost. No wonder she feels insecure.

The failing of her earthly father and other men change her consciousness. Now she knows the sin of judgment. Each failing man she meets fails, and she cannot help but judge him. This also breeds contempt.

But along with the judgment comes guilt for judging.

Without an understanding of what is really going on, she blames herself and then serves men out of guilt.

She hopes that her love and later her motivation will change him for the better. But it never does. Her love and support make men more wimpy and egotistical.

Her motivation only drives him to be more ambitious and fail or to be more rebellious and fail. There is no other choice.

Eventually he becomes married to his work or money, or finds another women to comfort his now more failing self.

Men--remember our example of the little bird and what the silhouette represents to the bird? Can you now see what a man's failing represents to the woman? It represents the original trauma. And it fills her with insecurity. So she might seek security in another way— the power she gets over the failing man, as well as the contempt and superiority she feels. She will also seek security in material things. Since none of these can ever truly satisfy, she continues to feel a terrible insecurity.

Men, now that you know the truth about man's original failing, perhaps you can now see why you must not blame the woman. It was the man's fault. Blame is just another use.

Instead, take responsibility and now see why you must not fail. You must not take advantage, nor must you use her to support your ego. See that drink, drugs, and ambitiousness are extensions of the original sin.

Most women come into the marriage with baggage: chances are her father was not there for her, and chances are someone used her. This past behavior of men awakened her to knowledge of disappointment, use, and then judgment and contempt, along with self blame.

That is why men will sometimes note that their wife is unhappy or acting angry or contemptuous after sex. To them it undoubtedly reawakens the ancient sense of loss and to a memory of a reinforcing experience of use and abuse.

Of course, procreation is necessary to bring children into the world. Thus it serves a good purpose. If you see that she is reacting very badly to sex, then you may have to go without for awhile, for her good (because you see the effect it has on her).

Remember to be respectful of her needs. Remember to love her as a person, not just for meeting your needs.

Tenderness, gentleness, and warm affection must accompany family making. Sex is not love. But it does not have to be use either. Let there be love (fatherly, agape understanding) in everything you do.

As time goes by and after the family has been formed, the husband becomes more fatherly. Sex diminishes, and despite what today's so called experts say, after the first few years of marriage enjoyment and after the children have come unto the world, sex is not necessary. Just don't force anything. Let it diminish naturally. It may surprise you to learn that most women have far less sex drive than men.

To the woman, sex often feels like abuse if she has been traumatized in the past. Therefore less sex, or perhaps no sex for a while, may be called for. Just make sure your abstaining is because you see the effect that sex is having on her, not because of resentment.

I have to say that it calls for the utmost in understanding, love, and wisdom to find the right measure in everything. That is why proper meditation (such as we teach at the Center for Common Sense Counseling) is helpful. What you do must be based upon soul searching and a deep commitment to do what is right. If it is done out of resentment, it will backfire.

You probably also see that the world is woefully misguided and in ignorance about what marriage, sex, and love are all about. As the father and husband, you must have wisdom and understanding. Do not expect others to have it. Remember: you must give love, not be out to get love.

Of course, if you wake up and begin to live in dignity and understanding, and if you begin to fail less, becoming more considerate, thoughtful and courageous, you family may respect you and perhaps love you. If they do, it is very good for them. Because they will be loving the good for which you now stand.

But don't have any expectations of what your newfound temperance and understanding may bring you. If you happen to have married a man hater (because when you picked her you did not have the understanding you now have), she will hate any newfound grace. She may do everything in her power to destroy you and turn the kids against you. You will have to bear it all with courage and without resentment.

If she truly hates the good she sees in you, she may go off and get a divorce. Just don't instigate the divorce yourself.

However, if in her heart your wife truly loves good and truth, then she may still try you. She may give you a hard time, accusing you of finding another woman or of being cold and uncaring. She may accuse you of becoming a homosexual. She may give you a hard time for years or even decades. Just understand what is going on. Don't resent her. Do your duty. Suffer in quiet dignity. Stay the course. Fight the good fight.

Stand for what is right. If what is right wins, then it is a win-win for both. Be firm about nonsense and naughtiness. Just take the resentment out of it.

If she sticks around and does not run off, there is hope. She may still give you a hard time when you are right, and support you when you are wrong. You may see glimmers of hope along the way.

A good marriage is a good fight. But when I say fight, I mean fighting for what is right. When what is right wins, then it is a win-win for both. Therefore, when you see what is right, hold your ground. But just make sure that you are right yourself. If she is right, then you must acknowledge it. And if you were out of order, then you must admit it and apologize for it.

Often the marriage becomes like the old expression: a Mexican stand off. She represents one world and he another. The line is drawn. If the man eventually wins, then she will one day willingly come into his heaven. If she wins, she drags him into her hell. (Of course, the woman might wake up first, and then her goodness will awaken her husband to either run off or to become better).

Let's say the man wakes up, realizes he is wrong. He quietly is sorry before conscience for his selfishness and pride. After a series of realizations (that can be quite painful at times), each time bringing pain, sadness, sorrow, even some tears, he begins to see how he has failed his wife and family. He sees how he has been blaming her; he sees the need to make some changes.

He mourns in private, keeping his inner repentance to himself.

Now he makes a short and simple announcement. He tells his wife that he realizes that he has been wrong and has failed her. He admits that he has been selfish and resentful. He apologizes to her and says from now on things will be different.

Note: never ask for forgiveness. Only God can forgive you. If you ask another person for forgiveness, it is elevating them to play God. This is not good for them. It breeds pride and contempt (and guilt before conscience if they do "forgive" you).

Instead apologize. Tell her that from now on things will be different. Keep it simple. Go about your business. Save any emotions or tears for your Creator, in private.

If the other person does forgive you—by this I mean drop their judgment and resentment—it is good for them. If they don't, it is not good for their soul. But whether they ever do drop their resentment or not is none of your concern.

Your only responsibility is to clear the air, admit your wrong (so they won't have a basis to judge you for continued pride). By admitting your wrong and apologizing, you make it easy for them to drop their grudge against you. But as I said, whether they do or not is none of your concern.

You may see surprising good coming from simply doing your duty, staying the course, and not resenting.

For example, your wife might be creating an argument or fuss over some trivial thing. Or she might be rebelling or being naughty in some sneaky way. You point it out, and she accuses you of being mean and harsh. So you continue to point out what you see, despite her confusion and accusations. You remain calm, kind but firm, and not resentful.

She may storm off and act like you are terrible. Just go about your business. Afterwards, when things have calmed down and the storm is over, she may act almost happy and almost glad. It could be a favorite ploy of the unrepentant--acting as if nothing happened.

But it could be that she is relieved that her naughtiness and confusion did not win and that you remained steadfast and calm!

She may see that she was out of order, and your holding fast to principle and not becoming resentful gave her a chance to recover. She may be glad to see you acting like a man for a change.

This type of thing is especially apparent with kids.

When dad says "no" to spending too much money, listening to rap music, or going out at night, they act like you are mean person. There will be moaning, groaning, complaining, and fussing. Don't pay any attention to it. You saw what was right, so don't vacillate. Just go about your business. Let the fussing and complaining go in one ear and out the other.

Often, after the storm has passed, you will see that they are secretly glad. Deep down, they knew they were out of order, but they could not stop themselves from wanting what their ego thought was its due. Now they are glad that dad there and dad was strong. When what is right wins, then all win.

Sometimes people need to be stopped--because what they are doing or what they want is not good for them.

But they need to be stopped not with anger and violence, but with a force call love.

A good analogy is the sports coach. A really superb coach is never angry. He or she is calm, kind, but has a firm but fair approach. The good coach does not need to yell or be angry. No good coach is a doormat either.

He is firm, strong, no-nonsense, and yes, he has to put up with complaining, moaning and groaning. (The "Coach, do we have to do push ups?" kind of thing).

Complaining is par for the course. He expects it but doesn't react. He just keeps doing his job.

By being calm, by not over-reacting, by not paying attention to the complaining, he wins the respect of the player.

Dear Dad, now that you have kids, it is too late to be selfish. Now you must be selfless. You must be steadfast and do your duty. But even more is required.

Many dads go to work, earn a living, provide for their family, take the kids places on weekends and so on.

This is all good. Just remember that you need to be there for your family as much as possible.

Ideally, the father is in charge of education, moral education, and correcting the kids. If one of the kids is out of order and you are speaking to them about it, there is nothing worse than to have a wife standing there cackling amen to what you say or throwing in her two cents worth. A man does not need support for what he does. Tell your wife that you can handle it, then deal with your child first, then later with her.

Dear husband: one day, your wife may awaken to see that you have become the noble knight she had dreamed of long ago. She will come to respect you. And if one day, she loves the good in you, then her soul will be saved too.

Don't take credit for any good. Realize that all you are just doing your duty. Any good that comes to pass is the result of grace now operating in your midst.

- 22 -

Dealing with Hard Times

Financial crisis does not have to lead to family crisis. Economic troubles don't have to result in relationship or health problems.

You can still be reasonably happy, healthy, loving, and cheerful in spite of external circumstances.

We all know this at some level. We have all heard that money can't buy you happiness. We've all seen families who have very little, but who have a lot of love. We've seen great men and women come out of poverty.

Many of us who are a bit older remember when we were young newlyweds, for example, and had nothing but a one room apartment, a lamp, a stereo, and some boxes to sit on. We remember that we were happy, much happier than years later when we had many material possessions.

Some of us have experienced getting what we wanted, having our heart's desire and yet feeling miserable and unfulfilled.

So if you know this, why do you get upset, worried,

distraught, and begin to have a churning stomach when you can't pay all your bills or when you lose your job?

The reason why is both simple and profound. First the simple sound byte version: you've permitted yourself to become upset over trivial issues. Thus you indulged emotions, and now when the bigger issues arrive, you are easily thrown out of control.

How can you remain calm in big troubles when you allow yourself to get upset by the little ones?

The simple solution is this: start to exercise what character you have left. Have some discipline. Be a man. Be a woman. Set a good example for your kids.

Don't indulge worry, doubts, and fears. Never take counsel of your fears, as a great general once said. Be patient. Remember: this to shall pass. Get busy, do something: go for a walk or help someone. Look for work. Volunteer. Forget self.

Pay special attention to and beware of anger which makes you wrong and guilty, and which conditions you to be reactive and out of control. See how judgment leads to anger. Let go of judgment.

Now the more profound reason why we permit external circumstance to affect our inner life, and by extension our relationship with others. We lack faith, and we have always been taught to look to authorities and external knowledge for answers. We are too externalized.

In other words, we look to the outside world for guidance. We look to the outside for support and comfort for our ego. And when we are not looking to others, we are looking into our intellect, hoping to dredge up some answer from there.

Where we should be looking is to intuition, what we ascertain wordlessly in the inner Light from God. But we avoid intuition. Because we have ignored it and erred, it now comes back as 20-20 hindsight. It feels like conscience and it makes us feel bad. And as long as we don't want to be sorry and admit our mistakes, we avoid feeling bad and shun conscience.

Of course, that is what just about everyone else is doing too. Can you see the folly of looking to some exert for guidance: an expert who is a prideful intellectual and who is devoid of conscience because he or she avoids conscience too? It is truly a case of the blind leading the blind.

But as I said, it is not totally your fault. You could not help inheriting the nature that is prone to being prideful. Nor could you help believing what everyone told you to do: get an education, look to authorities and experts for knowledge, be ambitious, set goals, and so on. You may have had a suspicion that there was something wrong with the teachers, educators, professors and experts' advice, since many of their own personal lives ended in failure.

But you did not grasp intuition (your hunch about such things) firmly enough. In your natural pridefulness, you wanted to get what you could out of life, and you went down the garden path to destruction just like everyone else, because you liked the false promises.

Without true faith, how could you argue with the lie that money and material possessions bring happiness; how could you argue with the seeming pleasure and materialistic benefits others were getting from working the system?

Yet, perhaps you suspected that all was not what it was cut out to be. You may also have seen examples of people who were industrious but not ambitious, who were principled and honorable and who succeeded without copping out, lying, cheating or tricking people.

You may have seen how the beautiful people, received the adulation of crowds and living lavish lifestyles were deeply troubled. Something just didn't add up. But you doubted your intuition or did not grasp it firmly and without waver.

Now it is not your fault that the culture in which you live does everything in its power to convince you that the answer to your problems is *out there* somewhere. We are told that knowledge is the answer and that the way to get knowledge is through sitting in dusty classrooms for years on end.

We are also told that more sex is the answer. We are always looking to some person to make us happy, cure us, or give us some secret to getting rich.

Advertisers, and particularly the chemical pharmaceutical companies, spend billions to convince you that the answer to your problems lies in pills.

We are treated like sheep, like children, even worse. We are treated as if we were animals: just chemicals, hormones, and stimulus response animals.

Until you fully grasp that you are a human being with a soul, and until you find the secret to the power of good available within to resolve problems, you will be at the mercy of those who lord it over you.

The answer is within. The answer is in learning to become objective and aware, functioning from intuition--the guiding of intuitive understanding and the protection of God's inner Light.

The answer is to trust more in your own God given intuition than in what others say.

So long as you look to the world for answers, for love, or for some sort of ego validation, you will remain tied to the world and dependent on it. You will become resentful when others betray you.

So long as you are externalized, when a change occurs--when the rain falls, the economy falters, or the customers aren't buying--you will become upset and frustrated.

Learn to go through life with equanimity. Do not become overly excited when things go well. Don't become crestfallen when they don't. Remember: "man does not live by bread alone, but by every word from the mouth of God."

Also remember that other people are lost too. Others are externalized. They have not found the answer. No one loved them enough to tell them the truth. No one had the understanding to share with them the inner path to God.

Therefore you must not hate other people. Many of us have grudges against our parents for not guiding us properly and for letting something bad happen to us.

Just remember: they could not give you what they did not have themselves. Also know that hatred and resentment cut you off from inner love.

Start by letting go of your resentments against others, beginning with those closest to you. Stop looking to the world for love and guidance. Stand back and observe.

Listen to what people have to say without reacting emotionally for or against them. When you read, don't get absorbed. Instead scan lightly for clues.

- 23 -

My People Perish For Lack of Knowledge

The words in the title are the words of God spoken through one of His prophets.

These words ring true down through the ages and are just as timely today as they were three thousand years ago.

Look into almost every family and you will see misunderstanding, resentment, judgment, anger, suppressed rage, cruelty, and suffering.

Every time you turn around, there is another divorce.

And when there is trouble in the family, those who hate traditional values and those who hate the family use the trouble to proclaim that the family doesn't work. Every time a father falls, it is used to say that men are no good, and that traditional values are just hypocrisy.

Every time mom or dad, husband or wife has problems, there are experts to step in and take away authority from the home.

The media, especially television, has for the last 30 years been mocking father, mocking the home, and mocking old fashioned values.

The church is under attack. And because some of the people who supposedly represent the church have made mistakes, it empowers those who would get rid of religion all together.

The knowledge we need to restore harmony in the home cannot be gleaned from books or classes. We need understanding about why men and women argue and fail. It is a mystery, but can be understood by anyone who sincerely seeks for truth.

It is an ancient and reoccurring cycle of rebellion against God. Just as in the Garden of Eden, the woman continues to be used by the serpent to entice Adam to turn his back on God. And both the man and the woman are then used by principalities and powers to rebel against the Creator and bring suffering on humans. Without understanding how they are being used, people continue to hate and blame each other.

Forgiveness is truly the answer. But we also need insight into the spiritual reason behind all the squabbling we see in families.

The family is the bedrock of civilization. The family is under attack. And the institutions that once supported the family, such as the church, have grown weak and decadent. The government, which once supported family, now has a welfare state in place that actually supports the breakdown of the family.

The relationship between the man and the woman, within the institution of holy matrimony ordained by God, holds the key to happiness, prosperity, and domestic tranquility. The family is the matrix in which the next generation comes forth, and it is the family which supports, nurtures and maintains the best of what it means to be a human.

But as I said, everywhere you look in the world--you see families boiling over with intrigue, betrayal, cruelty, suffering, and misery. Each and every couple started off expecting to be happy. But something goes wrong. We need to understand why.

Our families suffer for lack of knowledge. The one who is most to blame is the husband. It is his job to be the leader, the Moses, the David of the family. It is his job to be a man of impeccable honor, courage, patience, understanding, kindness, forbearance, and graciousness.

There is no way that he can be the man he needs to be unless he finds an invisible bond with the Creator Within. He must be so grounded in principle and faith, that there is no wavering, no failing, and no room for a lack of commitment to what is right.

He must be stronger than the world. But if he is woman centered--if women are the ground of his being and if his wife is his boss (or she lets him be the boss)--then he will not be grounded in good. Instead he will be a beast man, violent or wimpy, grounded in the woman, and beyond her in the serpent of old that tempted man through Eve.

My heart goes out to the decent women everywhere.

They are tempted to take change because of the weakness of the man. They are tempted by his weakness to support and console his prideful ego. Men require it of women. And when she gains power because of his nothingness and growing weakness, she is then called upon to nag him to get him to function.

When he greedily goes for her love offerings, first with excitement then with resentment, he becomes enslaved. And when he is enslaved by the temptation that he wanted from her, he is full of rage. The weak angry man goes off to another woman or to the bottle.

Perhaps he marries his work, or becomes enslaved to some other temptation such as gambling. Some men take on the woman's nature and become seducers in business or politics.

You see, the weak womanizing man never did love his wife; he loved the temptation he drew up in her.

All the while, the children are suffering.

Men need to have a thorough knowledge of their own weakness. They need to see just why they must not fail.

They need to see why they must be principled and honorable.

Women need to see that the Adam and Eve story is recreated over and over again. They need to see that, yes, most men are weak and failures. But she must learn not to resent them for it. She must see her own role in tempting him and rising to the occasion of his need, which made him weaker and gave her power over him.

She must see why she must not support him in his wrong, on the one hand, but must also not give him such a hard time that he doesn't have the space to find himself.

Perhaps a good starting point would be to realize that your husband is just a man, and judging and nagging him will only stand in the way of his finding himself.

Men, you must see that you must not look to your wife to support your ego. You must look to no one except your Creator for the strength, wisdom and understanding that you do not now have but will need if you are to be the kind of husband and father that your family needs.

And here's another tip: regardless of what your situation is, begin right now to be more forgiving. Drop your grudges. If others are wrong, see their wrong, but don't hate them for it. Let go of judgment. Make it unimportant. You yourself are wrong through your judgments and grudges. When you let go of bitterness and blame, you will then be free to see what the real truth is.

You may even discover the love from the Creator when you no longer look for love from others and hate them when they fail you.

- *24* -

Good Dads and Fathers – We Need Them More than Ever

Remember the line of the old song: "We're poor little lambs who have lost our way." I can't help but think that this describes most people in the United States today.

We have lost our way. Our families are falling apart. The schools are abysmal. Many people are eating wrong food. Many people are basically misguided.

Unfortunately many do not even know they are misguided. Their authority is no longer dad or husband, or even grandfather and grandmother. Their authority is some other entity, some big impersonal matrix working from its hidden abode, directing educators, experts, bureaucrats, and media which are now our authorities.

Mom and dad, a good Dutch uncle or someone with white hair and wisdom who the family has known for decades used to be our authority. They were real, and though they had feet of clay like everyone else, they were honorable and accountable.

Now our authorities are strangers. Who knows what kind of private lives they live and who knows what they say when not in their office or before the camera. Even the educator is a stranger.

We see our authorities on stage, in front of the class, or in their office. But we know nothing about them, their lifestyle, or what agenda they may secretly have.

It's sad really. My heart goes out to mothers who really and truly have to work, and who don't have a good mom or sister to leave the kids with. Instead she has to leave them with strangers.

So we are misguided and lost. Just because some expert said so, we leave the children with strangers. Just because some stranger said so, we don't get married. Or perhaps we turn our nose up on just being a mom, because a stranger said so. And just because some stranger said so, we take a chemical pill or give one to our child.

We do a lot of things because some stranger who claims to be an expert said so.

We do what the experts say to do, and when many things go wrong in our lives, we are even more lost than before.

If only father were strong and wise. If only he was the wisest person you knew. If only he were not himself a victim. If he were strong, courageous and graced with more understanding than anyone else in the world, then you could lean up against father and feel secure in his presence. You could ask his advice and he would help guide you to happiness, success, health and joy. If only His authority was infallible reason and love flowing from an inner bond with the Creator.

If only your husband were strong and full of love. If he was a man of impeccable honor, virtue, wisdom,

200

patience, and had the courage and conviction to stand for what he knows in his heart. You could look to him instead of strangers.

The family would be safe and secure. All would be reasonably happy most of the time.

Men, can't you see that your wives and children need you to be that man? If you are not the wise and just authority, they will look to others. They need you to be strong and to reach within to find the grace and wisdom that you will need to lead your family. You must be the Moses for your family. Your family needs you to be stronger than the world.

It's time for the men of America to step up. But don't wait for others to do so first. They may never. And don't look to your wife, support groups or other men to reassure and mother you along the way. Be a man and cry out to God. On your knees before the Father within. But stand tall before others.

Set a good example. Don't look for approval. Don't try to win a popularity contest. Be the man your family needs. Suffer alone. Be cheerful and light hearted. But put principle first.

Finally, don't pressure or force anything on others.

First make sure you are right, then let your authority be patience and wisdom out of love and understanding.

- 25 -

A Listener Asks

A listener asks:
"My Husband Irritates Me. I can't get him to change some bad habits that he has. What should I do?"

Dear Listener:
Thank you for your question. The first thing to look at is your own judgment and resentment. When we are resentful, we can be irritated by just about anything.

Next time you are upset or resentful, notice how sensitive you become. Just about anything--from a slow moving line to a change in schedule—can make you irritable.

In essence, resentment and judgment destabilize us because they cut us off from patience and love. The human being is more than just an animal. We have a soul. And the proper environment for our soul is truth and love. Not our truth or our love. But our Creator's truth-love.

By definition, when you judge another (with condemnation and unforgiveness), you have separated yourself from truth. Truth is understanding. It is impossible to have understanding and be judgmental at the same time. You must learn how to discern error without adding judgment.

When you resent another, you have also cut yourself off from love. God's love is a presence within the soul which you cannot usually know is there. But His love stabilizes our whole being. His love, though not palpable, restrains us from running amuck or from coming unglued and becoming hateful and nervous.

If you are like most wives, you have been judging men for a long time. Men are very judgeable and imperfect. At first, men's failings challenge you to try to change them. Their failings gave you a sense of superiority over them.

But soon judgment turns to condemnation, resentment, grudges and bitter memories. Worse yet, your judgment and secret resentment (which you call "hurt feelings") begin to change your beautiful nature into an ugly nagging and dominating one.

Observing these changes in yourself makes you resent your husband even more, since you blame him.

The bottom line is this: learn to observe your husband without judging him. See his failings, but don't hate him for them. Give him some space to be himself.

Chances are you are always critiquing, nagging, and wanting something from him. You pressure makes it hard for him to function.

It is just possible that there may be a real man in there somewhere. But your pressure disables him from functioning, leaving him angry and perhaps uncommunicative most of the time.

A man has to find himself. You cannot make a man into a man. Of course, it is also possible that there is no good in him. It is possible that he may be just selfish.

But you don't know for sure. Right now your judgment and resentment block you from seeing him as he really is.

We are told to be patient with others. Strange, isn't it, that we can be patient with strangers or coworkers, but find it impossible to be patient with those closest to us.

If you can't forgive and be patient with those nearest you, then something is wrong.

Patience does not mean resignation or acceptance with seething resentment. Patience means giving a person a chance. It means looking for the good in another. It means loving what is good in a man. And for men, it means loving what is good in the woman.

Of course, he is wrong too. His weakness, his animalness, his violence on the one hand or his wimpiness on the other hand tempted you and brought the worst out of you.

Basically, I have always said that when things go wrong it is the man's fault. He is supposed to be noble, honorable, principled, virtuous, brave, longsuffering, and full of wisdom and patience.

Alas your husband failed (as all Adams have failed their Eves). The secret to your recovery is in learning not to resent him. It matters not whether he ever becomes the real man you have needed or not. By not resenting him, you will free your soul to receive the love of God. As long as you resent and judge another, you block God's love from flooding your being.

A Listener Asks: What Is Love?

Dear Listener:

This, of course, is one of the most important questions in life. Most of us think we know what love is. We think we have love. And we think that what we feel for others is love.

We are shocked when our love is rejected by another (even our kids). We are shocked when our love, instead of making others better, makes them worse. For example, many a lady has thought that her love would make her oaf into a prince, only to see her "love" make him into an angry user or a wimpy slob.

Just look at what the government's "love" is doing to the welfare class. Look at what the public school's love is doing to the minds and scholarship of today's youth.

Look at what the entertainment media's love is doing to the caliber of the populace. Look at what the drug pusher's love is doing to the population.

A woman can feel when her husband's embrace is use of her. He calls it love, but it feels like abuse.

Therefore, despite all the love songs, romance novels and greeting cards, we, as individuals and collectively, must be missing the boat. Could it be that we don't really know what love is?

It could be and it is. If we had real love, then people would be happy, healthy, productive and free. Marriages would be harmonious instead of degenerating into a living hell.

If we really had love, then all the fighting, violence, divorce, alcoholism and drug addiction would be things of the past.

I must say: I cannot help the world. The world already has all the "help" it needs. There are plenty of experts, pundits, professors, writers, and helpers of all kinds.

There are more churches, more help organizations, more government social service agencies, more books, more support groups, more psychiatric meds, and more advisors and counselors that ever before.

If their help really helps—that is good. But the increasing suffering, misery, crime, and divorce rates indicate that something is missing. Somehow the "help" is not really helping.

I cannot help the world, but I can speak or write the words that might wake a few people up to realize that they really don't know what love is.

Only when you admit that you don't know will you have the searching, sincere attitude by which you might discover what real love really is.

In this brief chapter, I can only give you a couple of clues. So here goes.

First of all, love is correction. When people are permissive with us, it makes us feels good; but it is not good for us. At times we all need someone to stop us from hurting ourselves. Not with violence and not with anger, but with a force called love. We can tell when someone cares enough to get involved.

Secondly, love must have understanding in it. When we were younger, people would sometimes give us good advice, but we rejected it because they were talking at us instead of to us.

True love is emotionless. It often has a fatherly quality to it. Love is selfless. We think we love others when we need them or when they make us feel good.

But real love does not need another and therefore does not use them. The drug dealer does not really love the drug addict. And though the drug addict may need the drug dealer, he does not really love the dealer.

Love has truth in it. Any relationship that begins with lies (which most do) is off to a bad start.

Love does not have hate in it. When you are impatient with your children, you have no love for them. When you judge and condemn your husband, you have no love for him. When you resent your wife, you have no love for her.

Perhaps you can see that your egotistical state is naturally selfish. And we are never more selfish than when we are involved in emotions, resentments, and thinking. We are self preoccupied.

We need something to wake us up. Sometimes a noble person, the sweetness of a child, or a gracious act will awaken us from our selfish self involvement.

Perhaps a wonderful old movie or a real life act of selfless courage (such as a rescue operation) will awaken us to love. Sometimes a great tragedy or a close call will awaken us to remember what is really important in life.

But all too often we soon fall back into the comfort zone, the sleep of sin.

Only when we sober up from our emotional soup, stand back and observe things as they are, will we be able to love for the first time. And this love would not feel like love. It would feel like calm observation with concern (but not worry) for the other person. It would include a sincere desire to do the right thing along with the realization that you don't even know what the right thing to do would be. Wanting to do right but realizing your inadequacy (without resenting it) is the sincere cry of the soul. And it is answered by the Creator.

The Creator's love is first felt as conscience. It is a delicate wordless inner knowing. It makes us feel bad when we see our wrongness. But we also see in our Creator's inner Light that we cannot make ourselves right. This sober seeing becomes sadness, and the sadness becomes mourning, as our soul weeps in regret.

Soon the sadness gives way to gladness, as a right relationship with conscience returns. Before you know it, a situation arises where before we would have done or said what would have supported our ego. This time, we see what the result would be. And we find ourselves not doing or saying the selfish thing.

We find ourselves loving by not hating, loving by not using, and loving by not taking advantage. And this not of ourselves, but by the power of God.

- *26* -

Adam & Eve: The First Dysfunctional Family

Every so often I like to write an article or give a lecture about basics. So here goes. Today my son and I went to play golf. At one of the tees, there were many beer bottles lying on the ground that hadn't been cleaned up yet. I marveled at why anyone would want to drink so much.

But it then dawned on me that they were after a high.

People who drink, take drugs, engage in rituals, chant for long periods, and get lost in music are all after the same thing: a high.

Some people don't even have to take drugs or engage in a weird ritual. They can experience the high of hate, the high of using another or the high of arousing a crowd or audience.

In fact, most people get their high through emotions. They revel in their rage, bask in their excitements, and wallow in their self pity. Soon they degenerate to wallow in their pleasures and finally in pure pain.

You've heard the term "consciousness expansion?"

Now you know what it is they are after—to feel like God and to have a big expanding ego, without the restraint of conscience or reality.

Your friendly neighborhood transcendental meditation practitioner, guru, or drug pusher who talks of expanding consciousness won't tell you that they are trying to play God and feel like God, but that's what they are doing. And they want to corrupt you or your kids, making it all sound new and spiritual.

What is this high that humans are after? It is a state of having one's consciousness separated from God. At the same time one feels a sense of power or greatness, uninhibited by conscience or humility. The crack cocaine user is just getting this high faster. For a brief moment he feels powerful like God; but then he comes crashing down and feels like hell.

Whether driving too fast, drinking too much, working too much (to prove something or to escape from home), abusing their bodies, or upsetting others—the person gets a high from being liberated from conscience and doing something wrong, foolish or dangerous.

There is a high from shocking people. There is a high from punishing or abusing oneself. There is a high from power over others.

Teens and kids who drink alcohol, puff on marijuana or sniff glue are repeating the age old quest for the high. In their case, though, it is most likely to escape from guilt for resenting their parents or to escape from the boredom of school.

It often begins with being introduced to it by so-call friends, but then it becomes the easy escape from conscience or boredom.

Kids are often angry at their parents—especially when the parents have been impatient, accusatory, or haven't been there for them. Abandoned to the peer group, the kids become addicted to the group and guilty for giving up on principle. So they drink or smoke to escape from the guilt for hating their parents and copping out to peer pressure.

Other kids, such as the ones in college, are often guilty for being ambitious, for copping out to the pressure to study and become something (other than what God intended).

Maybe Adam experienced the first high. His heart started pounding as he reached with anxiety and excitement for the forbidden fruit. Maybe it was an apple, because there is a high just from doing something very wrong, but it might just as well have been mescaline, LSD, or crack cocaine). When he ate it, his consciousness became separated from God.

Liberated from God and the straight and narrow, he ventured into the forbidden. It was exciting for a very short period.

He did get high and felt like God for a few moments.

But then he came crashing down to reality. He saw what he had done, sensed that he had changed, and sensed that the rapport he had had with the Father was gone. He was traumatized.

As you may know, anything you take note of in the trauma scene can later affect you like the whole scene and carry you back to it. (I read of one man who returned from a Japanese slave labor camp after WWII, and was doing well until a waiter brought him a bowl of rice. He immediately went wild because a bowl of rice had been in the prison trauma scene).

In the original trauma scene, Eve was there. And to this day a woman has an effect on the psyche of man by her mere presence. Adam's consciousness was altered, and now he saw her in a different way.

He blamed her as if it were her fault. He blamed her and used her. And it became her loathsome duty to support him in his fallen, animal, degenerating state. She had been used by evil and now by her husband.

She undoubtedly resented her husband for having lost paradise, and her guilt for resenting him drove her to try to make up for it by supporting his ego.

For Adam, her presence was now a comfort and a distraction. He and his progeny wanted to forget the ignoble fall.

Now his progeny began to look for a high without shame. Some them still wanted to get high and feel like God. They believed the lie that through reaching for the forbidden fruit of knowledge, they could be gods.

Others sought to get high in order to escape from conscience, from boredom, and from the pain of the reality they now lived in. The high sets aside uneasiness over our fallen condition, reality, common sense, and the inhibition of conscience.

The first high seekers, and their modern counterparts too, also developed a habit of escaping into the imagination. There they can pretend they are great and good. We can forget, for short while, the failing state we live in.

The first high is feeling like God. The next high is to try to re-experience the first high and to escape from the guilt for the prior high.

But each time, the high is less high. More drug or shocking experience is needed to separate us from the inner light, from conscience and reality. Soon big doses of excitement, emotion, or drugs are needed just for maintenance. Soon the idea is not to feel like God but to find relief from guilt and pain.

Most of us have also been corrupted by emotions and feelings. Somewhere along the line we were emotionalized. Emotions give us feelings to escape into and emotions affect our consciousness like a drug.

Drugs are a substitute for emotion. Many people can escape reality and wallow in feelings without needing any drugs or alcohol. Emotion washes away reason when we get carried away. Emotions help us do what we want ambitiously or angrily, without the constraints of conscience. People turn to drugs and alcohol when emotion is not enough to totally escape from conscience, anxiety and reality.

Who of us hasn't gotten good and angry, storming away self righteously? And who of hasn't known the high of being in love or the depths of depression when rejected?

Up to a point it's normal. As kids we love to watch scary movies, laugh at comedies and get excited at sports events.

But at a certain point we begin to see that our emotions are not good for us. A big fright can traumatize a person and imprint them with a memory they can't shake. The memory affects the rest of their life, making them afraid of cars, afraid of dogs, afraid of people, or of telling the truth. The emotion of fear invoked by the memory of the trauma, in these cases, paralyzes and restricts the victim.

If the person uses another emotion (such as anger) to over-ride the first or uses alcohol to become disinhibited so as to function—they remain subject to the secondary emotion or the drug as well as a slave of circumstance and feelings.

Even as kids we could see the dysfunctionality of emotions. We saw our parents fighting, our dad getting angry or our mom becoming moody and unhappy. We knew there was something wrong with it.

And when we grew up and got married, we discovered, to our dismay, that anger, resentment, and hurt feelings began to ruin our home life. We had become emotionalized, and now through conditioning and having become externalized, we did not know how to function or live without emotions.

Next we discover the physical toll that run-away emotions have on our bodies. Diabetes, heart trouble, stroke, high blood pressure, migraine headaches, ulcers, colitis, and other symptoms are contributed to and may even be caused by emotions. While it is true that conditions can stem from purely organic reasons, a large percentage of our physical woes have something to do with emotion, especially excessive emotion. Even being prone to catching colds can have something to do with the body being run down from being upset and stressed out.

Since few of us have to run from wild animals, as our ancestors did, stress is mostly our *emotional* reaction to the pressure of others.

Now here is the basic point I'm making in this article: *we were not intended to be emotional. While emotions are part and parcel of our fallen existence, we were meant to gradually transcend them and become calm and dispassionate.*

Nor were we meant to be traumatized. Adam was not subject to evil until he responded to its wooing. It found his secret ambition and lack of commitment.

When Adam doubted God, he obeyed and became subject to evil, and in the process he was traumatized.

We, his progeny, are born subject to failing parents, and the whole human race is subject to evil. Today's pressures to be ambitious and to acquire raw knowledge to lord it over others are shades of the serpent's words about becoming a god through knowledge. Today's crack cocaine, marijuana, and other mind altering legal and illegal drugs are just modern variations of the apple.

The difference between us and Adam is that he had a choice, but we are born already subject to evil. Adam saw evil's seductive side, but when evil can't seduce us with dreams, perks and promises, then it stakes its claim through cruelty, violence, rape, betrayal, and war.

Evil is still around, operating through unaware people, seducing us with drugs, sex, music, and the promise of power or party time. It is there with a permissive logic, helping us to dream the impossible dream and then soothing us in our failing and offering something to take away the pain.

When we give in and partake of its offerings, we are traumatized and changed.

But once evil ascends to power, it does not have to seduce with pleasure anymore. It traumatizes with cruelty, betrayal and violence. Mayhem and violence are quick routes to shock and trauma. We are then corrupted by our hatred of the betrayers and those who abused us. Through hate, we become separated from love.

At some level, we do realize that the way to remain mentally and psychically safe is to remain calm. We all admire someone who is cool and calm under pressure.

We like our airline pilots and surgeons to be in control. We like our parents to be stable and predictable. We like them to be reasonable. We quite properly distrust people who are out of control in any way.

We are also wary of the quiet ones--those who repress emotion. On the surface they appear calm, but underneath they are seething volcanoes.

We must find the way to return to being centered and find a way to no longer over react to temptations and those situations, substances and people who represent and continue to trigger our emotional reactions.

As we outgrow the excitements of childhood and the passions of youth, we must become more reasonable, stable, and calm.

We must gracefully give up the pleasures of youth and become stable and measured in our ways. Most importantly, we must learn to give up resentment, the emotion of pride. As long as we think we are entitled to it and exercise our "right" to indulge it, we must suffer its destructive effects on self and others.

We must wean ourselves of emotion. I know this goes against the grain. We have all been taught that emotion is normal and we have been encouraged to cheer and scream, get angry and upset. We have been taught to drum up emotion to spur us on the victory over the other team. But when one team wins, the other is bummed out.

We must find the way to remain naturally calm—not by becoming cold and unfeeling, nor by repressing, nor by becoming numb. We must learn how to be steady naturally: reasonable and gracious in all circumstances, and cheerful most of the time.

Though we be people of peace, sometimes life requires that we act boldly, even with force. But what prevents many of us from acting decisively is the fact that we are paralyzed by the emotions of fear, or else we are afraid of speaking up because the emotion of anger makes our words come out wrong. Paradoxically, by being timid, we actually embolden wrong.

If you can learn to meditate with the right intent, you will soon discover that you have been an emotion addict. Proper meditation will help you stand back and observe people, places, and things with calm objectivity.

You will discover that it's not necessary to build up a head of steam to act. Without excessive anger or emotional blocks, you'll be free to be truly productive.

Proper meditation will also help you stand back from the fantasy in which we become immersed when we become emotional.

You will discover that another emotion—resentment—has affected and perhaps even ruined your life. Resentment is a sneaky high, one that involves secretly hating others and rejecting good. It makes us bitter, hostile, and guilty.

Every emotion has its backlash. Because emotion is an extreme reaction, it bypasses the center. It swings us to one side; and then to compensate, our bodies swing us to the other. That is why the high is always followed by the low. And the emotion that has the worst backlash of all is resentment. It leads to self hatred, morbid thoughts, depression and bitterness.

Therefore, it would behoove you to consider whether you should take advantage of your "right" to get excited, upset, or resentful. Consider the consequences of your indulgence.

In a moment of anger, some of us have said something that we regretted the rest of our life. Others of us, basically decent, are troubled by the thoughts we have when we are resentful and angry. We don't know how to control our emotions so we bottle them up, clam up, become a doormat, and eventually become sick from the repressed emotions.

By practicing the proper meditation, you can learn how to stay calm in the moment of stress. When the moment has passed, you are free to express yourself without excitement or resentment. And what you say will be truthful and neither too harsh nor too mild.

Many of us are capable of being calm when dealing with work or business matters, but when it comes to our own personal lives, we get upset and blow it. This is mainly because of the emotion of resentment, which leads to extreme subjectivity. Resentment and upset throw us into emotional thinking, where we tend to dwell upon the negative and wallow in misery.

Once again, the right attitude (one of wanting to know the truth and being willing to acknowledge our own wrong) coupled with the proper meditation will permit you to calm down and begin to see the forest for the trees. Life will not be boring. It will be quietly exciting. You will know the delight of discovering and realizing truth. You will joy and sweetness. And you will know peace. Not the eerie peace of separation from Reality and God, but the peace of reconciling to conscience and becoming a friend of God.

- 27 -

Ego Problems

Can you see that we want to be our own gods? We want a life apart from God in order to do our own thing. In order to have this exciting, risky life apart from God, we need support. God will certainly not support us in a disobedient life apart from Him.

So we must begin responding and getting involved in people, places, things, and substances in such a way that they support our ego.

Remember, the ego, because it wants to exist apart from God, must draw some sort of life energy apart from God, and it must also get feelings of life from people, objects and substances.

On a purely biological level, the fallen man and woman, having inherited the life that leads to death, must draw energy from their own diminishing storehouse. Early in life we glean enough energy from nature and from food. But as we grow older and more corrupt, we must stoop to lower and lower practices to generate feelings. We even become tempters ourselves draining the life from those we tempt in order to feed our ego which drains the body.

Originally Adam and Eve were intended to live forever. Their life came from God. Even as a plant lives in the sunlight, so the spiritual man is given spiritual life by his Creator. The soul, receiving life from God, is then able to give life to the body.

At the present time, the natural fallen human draws energy from food and from interaction with nature.

When our given storehouse of life force begins to be depleted, some ghoulish people go on to draw energy from the storehouse of other humans. When you are around some people, you feel drained. Now you know why.

It is natural that we get energy from food. But at best it supports our fallen existence. Perhaps if we live long enough—not being felled by accident or risky behaviors, and not succumbing to disease—we might live long enough to discover the secret to living forever.

The Israelite people were sustained by manna in the desert. Christ said that He had manna which we know not of. God does sustain His own, and for those special few who love Him and find salvation, He may one day provide them what will permit them to live forever.

This is speculation on my part, but I think that it is possible even now to live forever in the flesh here on earth. But this is not for everyone, just for certain ones.

Though perhaps one day, all who find salvation may do so.

Most people will die without finding salvation, and many prematurely. As I said, all we inherit is the fallen life that leads to death and the *possibility* of a salvation from it. But for this possibility to occur, we must love the Truth with all our heart and search for it with all our heart.

The life that we inherit, the fallen existence, is all we know. Most people do not search for any other because they do not yearn for any other. The life of pride is the life of excitement, and most of us are unwilling to let go of it.

By responding to temptation objects and tempting people, we get the excitement that feels like life and we get the false hopes that keep us looking for a false salvation for our ego. Perks, promotion, and a sense of false righteousness are what we want.

We want to be like God, feel like God and imagine ourselves great like God. To do so we need temptation to respond to and lies believe. We need something shocking to pull us away from reality, so we can dwell in the imagination and hide from the incriminating light.

Then we need more temptation, emotion and lies to help us forget that God exists--we need emotions and drugs to distract us and help us ignore and become unaware of our conscience that keeps trying to inform us that we are not God.

So we respond to people and objects that appear to offer what our ego desires. This response, this emotional response, is the excitement that makes us feel alive.

Whether it be the promise, the presence of the tempting person himself, the words, or some object or experience that represents the dream of glory—we respond. And when we do respond, we unwittingly establish that tempting person or object as a support for our ego.

Thereafter, we need that promise or presence.

Without it, our soul is exposed to its emptiness and shame. When the support is withdrawn, our ego feels empty and stricken.

Some people live on the approval of others. When that approval is withdrawn, they feel terrible. Others need the constant reassurances of others.

Many people need the material objects they have come to require. Still others use food, alcohol, pills, or drugs for the support of their ego.

You see, we are spiritual beings. And ultimately our support must come from a spiritual source. When we are children, our parents suffice. We are close to the Light, and so we see in that Light. There may be a protection that attends us, which at certain times gives us a very strong sense of danger or a strong inner press to avoid something or someone dangerous. At other times it may just delicately and wordlessly lead us away from danger or along a proper path.

As children we also have a strong sense of conscience. We know when something is wrong and we feel bad when we do wrong. Little do we realize that this is our closest connection with God. This rapport with what is true and what is good, which we wordlessly sense within, is the most precious thing we have.

Yet, though we may love what is right or though we may dislike injustice, we do not know that our conscience (what we wordlessly know in our heart) is our precious connection with God.

As far as relating to people, we relate to our parents and look to them for guidance. And this is fitting and proper. When parents are decent and when they confirm what we know in our hearts, we have no conflict.

Our troubles begin when we are made to accept something that conflicts with our intuition. We are often told to accept something because someone else says so—because teacher says so, for example. Even being told to accept something just because any authority (even our parent) says so conflicts with intuition. When others say something, we should not have to accept it unless we see that it is so. When we see that it is so (because we sense that it is right in the

222

Light of our inner intuition), then we go along with it because there is no inner impediment.

Remember, there are two authorities. There is God and there is the external. God makes His will known to us individually, by way of inner intuition. This ability to perceive, to realize, to know deeply, and to intuit is from God. When we doubt it, turn out back on it, or disregard it, we then come under the authority of the world.

Parents must realize that their responsibility is to protect their child from untoward influences and pressures. Their responsibility is not to create little robots or wind up toys, but to confirm and validate on the outside what the child knows on the inside.

Parents must remind their children of what the child already wordlessly knows and otherwise set a good example. That way, the parent (or other authorities) do not come between the child and his or her wordless inner knowing from God.

Sadly, most parents believe it is their job to force "being good" on the children and to demand obedience and respect. In this matter, they become agents of the world, separating their child from his common sense, creating conflict, and training the child to obey outer authority.

At best, the demanding parents create rebels or conformists (both of whom therefore have conflict with conscience).

In the Garden of Eden, Adam harkened to the voice of his wife. He doubted God and believed her serpent inspired words. This effected a change in allegiance.

Adam became subject not to God, but to his wife and the spirit that stood behind her.

To this very day, we are subject not to God but to mother, wife, and the extensions of the woman who embody the seductive worldly spirit: educators, big pharma, seductive false preachers, and politicians. They motivate and cater to our egos by accepting us just the way we are and offering promises of greatness. Then they comfort us and solace us, understanding our needs and offering another round of service to our egos.

They all embody the lying seductive spirit that eggs us on to dream of greatness and glory apart from God.

They promise us a worldly paradise based on knowledge. And because we are subject to the spoken word, we harken to their lies, we believe, and we follow them to our ruination. And when we become ill and broken, they rise with more lying symptom removal and consolation to finish the job.

The wages of sin are death, says the Good Book. Our sin is believing and worshipping those who build our ego up and then "save" it.

We turn our backs on common sense and what we know in our heart of hearts. When we are led into trouble, we again turn to worldly leaders who promise a cure. They call for more education, more study, and being more ambitious. We again listen and follow. And when we develop various mental, emotional and physical problems, they promise salvation through more knowledge: psychology, medicine, or pharmacology.

When we turn to religion, alas, more worldly ones, masquerading as true helpers arise. Instead of restoring us to conscience and intuition—so that we might become whole within—they offer more word study.

Always the seduction is words: the spoken word and the written word, perhaps embellished with music, when what we really need is to be restored to the wordless Word in our heart of hearts.

Many speakers, whether teachers or preachers, may be sincere. But it takes a special quality and a special disinterested love to speak in such a way that the words convey true meaning and restore a person to their own inner ground of being. There can be no guile or any self interest in the speaker, otherwise the listener will remain a prisoner of the words and is likely to get caught up in an unhealthy way with the speaker.

Because we are all subject to words, we are in fact subjects of words and slaves of sin. We cannot free ourselves. Mere words, no matter how flowery or how accurate, cannot save us. It is the Spirit of Truth that saves, and only when the words of the speaker are guileless and the soul of the listener receptive.

Solomon said that much learning is a weariness of the flesh. Have you ever noticed how rituals, speeches, and yearly reenactments are the same thing over and over again? They seem dead, unable to go beyond the sameness. Those who make the speeches or preach the sermons are always looking for some ego appeal, some new angle or hook to get people excited and caught up.

We need to be saved from having to go back over and over again to clever spectacles devised by man.

We need not the spoken word but the unspoken word, the Light from God, to enter our hearts from within and change us.

The best any speaker can do is to awaken a person to the Inner Wordless Word. Awakening to Truth and real meaning, the person is restored to wholeness, to an inner rapport with the Father Within.

We are born incomplete. As our life progresses, we become more worldly. And the worldlier we become, the more we are made of the world and in the image of the lying personality that stands behind it.

We are born close to the Light. But as we respond to the tease and challenge of the world, we begin to become more made of the world and more answerable to the world. With each corruption, we become a little less like what we might have been by responding to the inner Good. We become less and less responsive to conscience and the world of principle that conscience represents.

Can you see why struggling with our external responses does not help? Of ourselves we can only be more and more answerable to the world which continues to tease and challenge us. Even when we resent the world or when we struggle resentfully with our failings, we remain subject to that with which we struggle resentfully. You cannot save yourself.

The answer is to find and respond to the inner world of Good, which we now know as conscience or a vague anxiety. The Light from God contains all that we will need for our return back to Him. The more we respond to the inner Light, the less we respond to the external tease.

The soul is capable of giving power to the body. The senses are used by the soul, and through the senses the soul perceives what is going on in the world. And the senses are attuned to and responsive to what the soul gives them power or direction to.

The lust of the eyes and the lust of the flesh have everything to do with the soul's illicit desires or misguided attentiveness.

For example, have you ever noticed how if you buy a new car, you begin to see cars like yours all over. Before you didn't notice them, now you do. Have you heard the expression that people see what they want to see and hear what they want to hear? When you learn a new word, then you begin to see it where before you never saw it.

This is the power of the soul to perceive and discriminate using the senses, and now reflected in what the sense are attentive to, fascinated by, or responsive to.

Food tastes better when you are hungry. Your eyes notice water fountains when you are thirsty.

Now, when the soul yearns for love, if that yearning is misdirected from God to other people, then the senses will pine for or lust for what the soul thinks will be its fulfillment. Some people (especially women) look to food for love. Their hunger will increase and it will be a hunger that is never satisfied because of the soul's pining for love.

Now, just as the soul directs the sense through its inclination, yearning or desire, the soul gives power to the senses.

Without the soul giving the senses power, they are dead. Can you now see why struggling with our addictions or compulsions only makes them stronger?

The soul's directing its attention to some external fulfillment through the senses vivifies, electrifies, and intensifies the senses. This also occurs when we resentfully direct our attention to some unpleasant thing. The soul's resentful attention intensifies the sensations, increases the pain, and strengthens the hold on us.

Remember the principle—the soul gives power. That is why if you resent and struggle with anything, it gets stronger. That is why we must not struggle with compulsions, ideas, or even voices. This is also why we must not struggle with other people. They literally take your power.

What then to do? Learn to observe calmly, with a little bit of distance between yourself and what you are observing. Learn to observe your own reactions objectively, without adding another layer of reaction to what is already there. Learn to observe other people without responding emotionally, excitedly or resentfully to them.

When the soul stands under God, its authority is the Creator. Having faith and love, it stands back and observes people, circumstances (and even its own wrong reactions) calmly and neutrally. By not reacting, the soul no longer gives more power to wrong, to error or to its own reactions.

By having faith it calls upon the Creator when faced with situations and problems that must be dealt with.

Having love (patience), it does not judge and take resentment and excitement energy from observing other's errors. It trusts in God to show it what to do, if anything, and it trusts that God will deal with the situation it is confronted with.

- *28* -

Recovery: Finding the Way Back from Naughty to Natural to Innocence

The so-called natural attraction we have for other people and for things starts off innocently enough, but soon becomes unnatural As kids we are attracted to play, learning, toys, nature, our parents, other kids, and food to eat. This is perfectly natural and wholesome.

We need love, which we get from our parents; we need activities for learning and discovering. And so nature itself, sports, and reading are attractive to us. In other words, we naturally love to play, love our parents, love to relate to other kids, love nature, and love learning.

However, as humans we are also capable of responding to truth or lies, to truth or deception, to what is right or what is wrong, to the good or to temptation. What happens is that lies and liars use the natural to get to us, and take advantage of our natural attraction to something wholesome or needed. They add a little lie, a little corruption to the natural. And without realizing it, we are taking in something harmful and unknowingly becoming conditioned to accept that unnatural little extra.

When a little corruption, a little lie, a little unnatural is subtly added to the natural, we gradually become habituated and accustomed to its presence. An innocent person of by-gone days would be taken aback by and abhor boorish behavior or four letter words. Today we are accustomed to bad behavior and foul language. It came through the music, the video games, movies and television (that were once innocent and natural).

A mother can subtly (often without even realizing it) turn the child against dad by conveying her resentment of her husband along with the food and maternal consolation. A school system can use children's love of learning to add a little indoctrination of some agenda along with the 3 R's. A food company can put a little m.s.g. in the cookies to increase usage and loyalty. The deceit in a seducer or advertiser can use words to suggest something that is not true.

In the Garden of Eden, the serpent used Eve and used the food to convey a lie. Thus something natural is subtly altered by a hidden message or substance. And as we take in the natural, we also take in the unnatural.

Once we become used to it and comfortable with it, we will crave more of the substance of the lie because it makes us feel good. Once corrupted, the natural makes us uncomfortable. As we begin to fee guilty (and not knowing why), we gravitate toward the corruption and feel ashamed and uncomfortable in the presence of the innocent and wholesome. We may yearn for it, but feel unworthy of it.

230

The purpose of this writing is to awaken you to see what has happened. When you see the deceit behind the lies you have believed, you will be able to doubt them, and then with a change of heart, begin your journey back to innocence and wholeness.

When we are close to the truth or the good, not responding to temptation in other words, we hardly even sense its presence. It's more like the sun is there making light for our eyes to see. We don't look at the sun. Similarly, the Light of Truth shines on things so we can see what is. It's not so m much saying "this is truth and that is false," so much as it is seeing *in* the light.

We don't talk about the sun as much as we talk about things that the sun illuminates.

When we respond to the Light of Truth, we are delighted and filled with joy over the discoveries we make.

But remember, we said that there is also something called deceit and falsity. And the source of deceit and falsity is temptation. When we begin responding to the source of temptation we begin to fall away from the Light of Truth.

This process happens to all of us in our lives, until the pain of our wrong causes some of us to cry out for salvation from lies.

Fortunately, some of us yearn to refind and respond to the Truth, and when we refind it, our love draws us even closer to it, so that we might see even more deeply.

As kids, we delight in discovering the marvels of God's great green earth. God wants the children to delight in things. We are close to God, and so our soul delights in what is natural for us.

But as we begin to get older, we begin to become exposed to temptation in various forms. Probably the first and most influential temptation in our life is our unloved and uncorrected mother. Alas, our dad married her for her temptation value. Her temptation was exciting to him, and soon she became the ground of his being. He married his temptation in other words.

Needless to say, he was set up for her temptation by his mother, who was the first temptation in his life. His mother was unloved (because her husband had married her for her temptation value). He, as the next generation of husbands, had no intention of correcting her for her naughtiness. It was her naughtiness that turned him on.

In exchange she got his life and gained control over him. Understand--I am not blaming mom. It was her husband's weakness and lack of love that tempted her to judge him and tempted her to rise to the occasion of mothering weak and wrong egos.

And so the unloved and uncorrected mother is too much for her kids, and she tempts them to respond to her temptation (seduction or bossiness) with resentment, rebellion or conformity.

The young ladies will find someone like their dad, whom they will be required to be a temptation to. The sons of the fierce mother and weak father will go out into the world looking for someone who excites them.

Bear in mind that some women do not want to be the temptress. They know they have to be one to catch a man, but they hope that he will become the knight in shining armor and no longer require them to be a tease.

Also bear in mind that many men are decent. They respond to temptation, but they would rather not. Deep down, they want to be the noble knight, but they just can't stop reacting to the confusion, naughtiness, and seductiveness of their wife (or their female imprinted bosses, ministers or politicians).

Now, as we go through life, progressively responding to temptation, first in our parents and later in others, we become increasingly shaped and molded by that temptation. We become reactive emotionally, we become resentful, and we develop various physical and mental changes and compensations as a result of adapting to those people and objects we are responding to.

That is why we change for the worse. That is why we gradually stop responding to the innocent things and ideals of youth. We start to become interested not in innocent pursuits but in some form of temptation. We become interested in raw knowledge, in power, in street knowledge, in drugs, in gambling, in naughty or nasty people. We become increasingly mortified and earthy, as we become more animal in the flesh. As our soul is downgraded through its growing enslavement to the spiritual temptation source (that stands behind the experiences), our flesh becomes adapted to the experiences through which temptation operated.

Can you see why a natural or wholesome experience, and one that is not a temptation, is not addicting? It's because we do not adapt to it. But when we respond to some sort of temptation operating behind an experience—be it excitement or comfort to our ego, a little buzz from an escape from conscience, a little high from praise, a little excitement from escaping from boring reality, or something to judge--we are altered. Our body, reflecting that change in allegiance and source of inspiration and motivation, becomes adapted.

It is not the drug that addicts; it is our response to the temptation it represented, that changes us.

That is why comfort can be just as corrupting as any other temptation. When we look for undeserved comfort (to deny the truth and pain of conscience, or to salve our tension from improper living), we are responding to temptation.

Can you see now why men become adapted and enslaved to women? It is because it was the female form through which temptation first operated in the Garden of Eden. Can you see why food causes change, decay, and why we misuse it? It is because we misuse it for ego comfort and entertainment.

This does not mean that we should give up marriage, food or any natural activity. It means that we must see that any problem we have involving some person, object or substance has to do with our having reacted to temptation operating through it. We began to change and adapt to it. And we continue to react to it and even to need it.

Even in something natural, we keep looking for the original nectar of temptation that we were injected with and touched by. Even if some object has no temptation presence in it, our bodies are addicted anyway. And we even try to call up or conjure up the temptation we once responded to.

Now that you have heard the downside, here is the upside. As soon as we begin to respond to the Spirit of Truth that stands behind the experiences of inspired words and the repentance experience, we stop responding to the spirit of deceit that we responded to earlier. We begin to change back, from the unnatural to the natural. A change takes place deep within the soul.

The body and its appetites are also altered, from the unnatural to the natural. We become more innocent and natural like we were as little children (except now mature), and somewhat as Adam and Eve were before their great fall. Years go by, as we live out our lives in innocence and humility. One day we take on immortality, as our flesh becomes imperishable.

The beautiful part is that a change for the better begins the moment we respond to the Spirit of Truth.

We sense the response in our physical being as a shock of recognition, perhaps sadness, as we recognize the truth about our wrong. We also sense it as a breath of fresh air, perhaps as joy, as we welcome Truth.

Next, approaching the same experience where once we responded with excitement or resentment to the temptation, we now see the truth about our wrong response. Now, responding instead to the Presence of Truth (in Whose Light we see the truth about our error), we change. Soon we are no longer compatible with the temptation, and we find that we no longer need the experience to support pride or our altered physical form.

Our being is upgraded by continued response to Truth, and we are able to effortlessly set aside our addictions. The first things to go are the latest to appear in our descent. Therefore gross habits and addictions such as drugs, cigarettes, alcohol abuse, gambling, or marijuana will be the first to give you up. There is little to do other than stand back and watch. Any effort on your part to improve yourself or to deal with hang ups only involves you more deeply with them.

Learn the discipline of simply standing back and observing. The mere fact that you are responding to the Inner Light (which is proved by the fact that you learn to obey the Inner Light and stand back and observe without attempting to do anything) will result in a change for the better.

Your body will once again learn to respond to the Inner Light. You will simply find yourself incompatible with those things your soul once needed for distraction and your body for stimulation.

The first to go will be the latest to appear. Included in this category are drugs and alcohol abuse. Like magic, you will no longer need them, and they will just give you up.

You will then be free to observe other wrong reactions and misuses out of existence. First the Light will make you aware of a wrong practice or reaction.

Seeing it, you will feel pain as you observe your own wrong and also your own helplessness to make yourself right. The Light will repent your soul and then you will be able to see the reasons why the reaction or practice is wrong. You will be given to power to quietly say no to the old practice or compulsion.

You will be given private counsel and understanding. After this experience, you will be free to approach the old situation, this time with detached objectivity and free of the hold it had on you. A similar circumstance will arise, and you will discover that you can handle it correctly.

You will find yourself becoming a more natural person as your gross habits and over-reactions give you up. One by one, layers of wrong will peel away. As the months and years pass, you will approach closer and closer to the oldest traumas that set you on the path of destruction. There is no telling what you might encounter, as it is different for every person. In general, the newest go first and the oldest last. It is for this reason that food and sex practices, though modified along the way for the better, will be the last to be perfectly dealt with.

This is because these practices are our individual and collective life supports for survival, and are intimately connected with an ego sense of pride to maintain us in our fallen condition. Food in particular is connected to original trauma in the Garden of Eden. Because we must eat to live, the lie and the human race's memory of the trauma is contained and reinforced in the mere act of eating.

Food was undoubtedly connected to our earliest traumas as individuals. Through food, the temptation operating in mother staked its claim on the child. When we ate her food, we also responded to that part of her that wanted our loyalty and to do her will. When we ate her food, we did her will and took in her suggestions.

Some children rebel against the food pressure, but their anger or aversion (and subsequent guilt) also result in a trauma.

Remember the basic principle: when we respond to the spiritual temptation operating through the trauma experience, we are imprinted by both the spiritual temptation and the experience. In the twinkling of an eye, our soul falls from its safe abode of calm distance and neutrality, and as a result, the body is left open to have to react to the outer circumstance. The mind is opened to react and respond to the suggestions and directions stated or implied in the experience.

In the trauma experience, we become a little bit like the trauma spirit, and physically we adapt to the trauma experience. The trauma experience becomes a new environment for our body to which it must react, adapt and find a way to feel comfortable with.

During the trauma, the imprinting occurs, a susceptibility to the suggestions takes place, and a growing familiarity with the corrupting experience begins. Simultaneously, the process of physical change begins.

It is the familiar spirit of the trauma that we are psychically drawn back to. We seek the spirit of our change and of our new mortal life of pride in every subsequent similar experience.

Men look for the spirit of the mother in their wife.

Women look for the spirit of the father who they hated and who failed them. But at a deeper level, the fallen person is looking for the spirit of temptation, the netherworld spirit that touched our soul and awoke it to pride, the excitement and pleasure of naughtiness and rebellion, the promise of knowledge, and the glow of pride or the high of hate.

Somehow in the temptation experience our soul was touched. And like the proverbial lady who bears her neck to Dracula, we return to the scene of the crime and bare our neck to the Dracula spirit.

At the mental level, we become subject to the hypnosis that occurs both because of the shocking effect of a traumatic person or circumstance (by which nature facilitates adaptation) as well as the suggestions that were made at the time. For example, if the suggestion was implied that mom's food is the best food, then we keep returning to mom's food because it is the best. If the suggestion is that her food is a comfort, then we return to that type of food for comfort.

At the physical level, the body is compelled to adapt to the new environment. Whether by flight, fight, passive tolerance or tiring resistance, the body is stressed by the trauma environment. It learns to read the trauma sources signals, deal with them, and make adaptations. And as the adaptations proceed, the day comes to pass when the body will need that trauma environment for stimulation, growth, and security.

That is why we come to love (need) that which we hate (trauma). We can grow to need the most loathsome dictator, we can need our awful junk food or beer, or we can need our work which we hate.

Can you see why many indiscriminate experiences are sure to lead to trauma and corruption? Parents who abandon their kids to the TV, to neighborhood socialization, to unsupervised or under supervised daycare, preschool and school environments are sure to open the door to corruption.

Can you see why it is not the junk food that cause aberrant or rebellious behavior, it is the spirit of trauma behind it or the suggestions involved?

A group of unsupervised kids can be sitting around and one brings some junk candy that parents forbid.

The excitement will overwhelm some and they will eat the candy with the excitement of doing something bad or forbidden.

Others will have been told by their parents not to eat junk food candy, and the pressure from the other kids and the desire to be accepted will overwhelm them and cause them to go against the will of their parents.

This is the trauma. Yet other kids might balk and say they don't want to eat the candy, but are criticized, ridiculed and mocked. These reticent kids might either resent the criticism (a resentment trauma) or cave in (out of doubting themselves because of resentment and guilt). This is another trauma.

Years later, the candy represents the initial excitement, being accepted, as well as guilt (and then escape from guilt in the hypnotic eating of it) for copping out. Voila, a love-hate relationship with candy.

Then, of course, there are other suggestions implicit in the junk candy (or rock music, marijuana, piercing, and just about any temptation our young people are led into). The suggestions touch our pride with notions and promises of party time, pleasure, excitement, being cool and so on.

For the kids who become enamored of their teachers and coaches, there is often a spirit of temptation operating through ambitious teachers and coaches. They seduce the child's soul with notions of greatness and glory through knowledge or sports.

It's not the knowledge that is wrong, it is the spirit of temptation operating through those who themselves were tempted.

There is a spirit of temptation operating everywhere in society. It operates through the unloved uncorrected females, the wimpy or violent men, the plastic hypocritical society, the lying politicians, and the supportive social service agencies. It operates through the hand of man, whether purveyors of drugs offering symptom relief, the purveyors of feel good drugs, or the casinos.

The effect that a drug has on an aware truth loving person and one who is not aware is completely different. An aware person responds to the inner Truth rather than to outside deceit. The aware person is not likely to take a drug, but should he have a little drink that contains alcohol, for example, about all he might observe are some physical effects.

But the person who wants to escape from truth will welcome any effects and allow them to pull his consciousness down. An aware person might get a little happy and then sleepy from a little drink of alcohol. But the one who wants to escape will lose awareness and become more of the selfish, lustful, hateful, deceitful person he was all along.

His body will be totally at the mercy of the alcohol because his soul has stepped away from its first abode.

The alcohol will thus become the traumatic change agent that will render adaptation in the body.

It is for this reason that any kind of drugs given to a person who is not very aware will force the body to toil, be stressed and adapt to the stressor drug.

So there are two aspects to the addiction. There is the psychic need for escape and guilt relief; and there is the physical craving of the adapted body. Thus there is a psychic craving and a physical one. The physical one is actually easy to deal with, once the psychic need is gone.

By far the most important thing is learning to respond to the inner Light of Truth. This change of allegiance, repentance, and the subsequent modified relationship with thing gives the soul a fresh start.

Recently established unholy and unwholesome practices just fall by the wayside. The soul is no longer compatible with them.

Older and deeper compulsions and needs (involving food or sex, for example) are not immediately eliminated, but are modified and upgraded. Certain practices that we once used for escape or entertaining distraction will be seen in the Light and no longer needed by the soul. All that the person need do is watch the body's craving without struggle and without giving in, until the obstinate craving gives way.

We have fallen to need our poisonous environment, our poisonous drugs and our toxic relationships because our guilty and rebellious soul needed them for distraction, escape, and comfort.

First the soul believed the lie and the false promise it entailed. Then it partook and was corrupted. Then it needed the experience to deny the truth again and again, and to escape from guilt.

The soul that becomes a friend of the Light no longer needs distraction or escape. It is perfectly happy in God's reality, and is quietly excited by the discoveries it makes in the Light.

If you believe that what is wrong with you is merely physical and you believe that a drug can cure you, then you will take the powerful drugs they sell you. Your unawareness, misplaced faith, and departure from the inner Light render your body susceptible to alteration and adaptation to its drug environment. This will disturb other physical relationships, and a chain of changes and alterations will ensue. Each with its side effects. The physical and chemical changes are powerfully distracting. And the placebo effect might even make you imagine yourself to be better for awhile.

You might stop worrying, but eventually when the placebo effect wears off, you will discover that you have enslaved yourself.

Perhaps now you can see why men and women become locked into love-hate fixation to each other; and why, instead of cooperating and being good helpmates to each other, they can't seen to stop making each other unhappy.

Drug abuse, food abuse, work abuse, and our addictions and dependencies, even our subjection to hypocritical or dictatorial politics are all extensions of the original temptation in the Garden.

For this reason, inherently and psychically, and because we all had failing moms and dads—men and women remind each other of failing and falling. Each of us falls for another, then hates them when we see that we are worse off not better. Soon our fall makes us dependent on the other or their type of temptation.

Men need women to excite and support their ego. Women need men to judge and dominate for a sense of superiority.

Now that you know the truth, learn to overlook the error operating in other people. In other words, don't use the error in another to build your ego. Don't take advantage. Don't puff up in judgment.

By not using, you reveal love. The kind of love that does not take advantage.

Stop resenting. See and appreciate what is good in a man. See and appreciate what is good in a woman.

- *29* -

Coping with Manipulative and Controlling People

In order to be truly happy and truly successful without guilt, we must first look at our own inner life.

We must see that we have become resentful, judgmental and perhaps secretly hostile. We must first give up resentment and judgment. Only after we have given up resentment and anger, and only when we have given up judgment, can we then see clearly and move intuitively to live properly.

Another thing--some people try to change the environment in order to make themselves feel at ease.

They divorce, take a new job, or they try to change their kids, their spouse or even their parents. Such people will find that when they go to a new place, they take the same attitude with them. Soon they will be resentful and judgmental there, again feeling empty and uneasy because of the resentment.

Other cleverly cruel, angry or manipulative people dominate their family, making them walk around on egg shells—afraid of "upsetting mom," for example, or fearful of dad and his "short fuse." The dominant one is controlling. I can't list all the ways of being manipulative and controlling; but I can give a couple of examples so that you might look at your own situation and see who is controlling you (or perhaps you are the controlling one).

As previously stated, some people control others through anger, rage, or unpredictability. Parents or people in authority use this if they can get away with it.

Others use something they have on you, or use some guilt you have to control you. Many a wife will never forget her husband's indiscretion and uses it against him to keep him guilty and controllable.

Some use sickness or disability to control people.

Those around them are afraid of speaking up to the sick one, so as not to appear mean. Others use syrupy sweetness and a veneer of perfection. They are so clever at appearing so right and so nice, it is hard to pinpoint what is really going on. Some wives are experts at putting on the poor me martyr act--everyone is fooled except those in the family who experience her tyranny behind closed doors.

Some men are clever at putting on the whimpering dog "I'll never do it again" act. The wife feels sorry and accepts him back despite his bad behavior.

The underdog in any controlling relationship is often controlling too. He or she uses guilt to manipulate.

Sometimes the underdog will take a lot of abuse in order to then be freed to do or have what he or she wants. The abuser feels guilty and perhaps afraid of being found out, so he or she gives the victim money or lets him get away with things.

Then, of course, there is the guilt on all sides—guilt for manipulating and being manipulated, for living a lie, for conforming and appeasing. All are guilty and thus all are avoiding the truth.

Truth becomes the enemy because any truth would rock the boat and expose everyone. So you have the elephant in the living room that no one talks about.

Sometimes the most feisty and truth loving member of the family will speak up. Everyone then gasps and acts as if that person were terrible and mean. They might even accuse the truth- speaker of being crazy. In the conspiracy against the truth, the one who is honest is the outsider. In Communist countries, the truth speaker is taken to political prison or to re-education camp. Or perhaps declared insane and given shock treatments, drugs, or lobotomy.

In the family, the most likely one to be honest is the little child, who still sees clearly. That child may be beaten. Or perhaps more wicked and subtle techniques are used: such as rejection and confusion. Everyone sees it as their bounden duty to make the child conform to the cultural insanity and the family lies. Today, there is the cruelty of medicating the aware child with psychotropic drugs: putting a straight jacket on his soul.

All so that the cruel and truly disturbed ones might feel comfortable.

Now you know the truth. If you are one of God's own, you were like the ugly ducking who was really the beautiful swan. The world around you tried to convince you that there was something wrong with you. And because you became resentful and upset, they managed to get you off balance, confused, and guilty. That way, they could go undetected, while everyone was busy pouring over what went wrong with you.

Your recovery depends on realizing that there was never anything wrong with you. Your mistake was two fold. First you doubted yourself. Second, you became resentful. Doubt and resentment cut you off from your own inner ground of being. Thus you became subject to the cruel environment that made you off balance.

You become subject to the very ones who upset you in the first place.

The problem is that you went about trying to get free from the oppressive domination in the wrong way. You became resentful and angry. You rebelled. But not being firmly grounded, you looked bad, rebelled in a foolish or self destructive way, and faltered.

Now you know the truth. The whole world is stark raving mad. And sometimes the most cuckoo of all is a member of your own family, your mom for example.

The secret to not becoming nutty yourself is to see that others are a little crazy, but don't hate them for it.

And even more importantly, don't let them make you doubt yourself!

If you doubt yourself, then you may begin to think that maybe there is something wrong with you, and you will be dragged into their hell.

Watch out for the two big mistakes: becoming resentful, and being made to doubt yourself. Those with credentials and degrees, for example, specialize in doubt. They speak so knowingly and cleverly, you could begin to think that there is something wrong with you, and that you are wrong for not seeing it their way. If they don't bowl you over with a cascade of clever confusing words, then they might try drawing you into an intellectual argument.

Careful. State your point simply. But if you see that they are not sincere and are seeking to get you upset and emotional, then it might be best to just back away and let it go. If they can pull you into the intellect and then make you resentful, you will falter.

Stand back when you find yourself getting pulled into no-win arguments.

Don't get trapped into trying to win the argument. State your point and take leave if necessary. It can be a deadly cat and mouse game. The enemy (and those controlled by the lie) will try everything in their power to confuse and upset you. They might even try the reverse psychology of accepting you and lavishing praise on you. If you accept their false praise, you will again become guilty. Watch what they are up to, and don't resent them.

Begin each day with the meditation we teach here at the Center for Common Sense Counseling. Thereby you will be pre-armed with patience and mental distance. It will help keep you centered.

Can you see how faith (not doubting yourself) and patience (not resenting others) keep you immune from the confusion and cruelty of the world? Faith and patience put up a force field through which the bad cannot enter.

- *30* -

My Husband is Annoying

A listener asks: "My Husband Irritates Me. I can't get him to change some bad habits that he has. What should I do?"

Thank you for your question. The first thing to look at is your own judgment and resentment.

When we are resentful, we can be irritated by just about anything.

Next time you are upset or resentful, notice how sensitive you become. Just about anything--from a slow moving line, to someone's scraping a chair on the floor--makes you irritable.

In essence, resentment and judgment destabilize us because they cut us off from patience and love. The human being is more than just an animal. We have a soul. And the proper environment for our soul is truth and love. Not our truth or our love. But our Creator's truth love.

By definition, when you judge another (with condemnation and unforgiveness), you have separated yourself from truth. Truth is understanding. It is impossible to have understanding and be judgmental at the same time.

When you resent another, you have cut yourself off from love. God's love is a presence within the soul which you cannot usually know is there. But His love stabilizes our whole being. His love, though not palpable, restrains us from running amuck or from coming unglued and becoming hateful and nervous.

If you are like most wives, you have been judging men for a long time. Men are very judgeable and imperfect. At first, men's failings challenge you to try to change them. Their failings gave you a sense of superiority over them. But soon judgment turns to condemnation, resentment, grudges and bitter memories.

Worse yet, your judgment and secret resentment (which you call "hurt feelings") begin to change your beautiful nature into an ugly nagging and dominating one.

Observing these changes in yourself makes you resent your husband even more, since you blame him.

The bottom line is this: learn to observe your husband without judging him. See his failings, but don't hate him for them. Give him some space to be himself.

Chances are you are ever critiquing, nagging, and wanting something from him. You pressure makes it hard for him to function.

It is just possible that there may be a real man in there somewhere. But your pressure disables him from functioning, leaving him angry and perhaps uncommunicative most of the time.

A man has to find himself. You cannot make him into one. Of course, it is also possible that there is no good in him. It is possible that he may be just selfish.

But you don't know for sure. Right now your judgment and resentment block you from seeing him as he really is.

We are told to be patient with others. Strange, isn't it, that we can be patient with strangers or coworkers, but find it impossible to be patient with those closest to us.

If you can't forgive and be patient with those nearest you, then something is wrong.

Patience does not mean resignation or acceptance with seething resentment. Patience means giving a person a chance. It means looking for the good in another. It means loving what is good in a man. And for men, it means loving what is good in the woman.

Of course, he is wrong too. His weakness, his animal, his violence on the one hand or his wimpiness on the other hand tempted you and brought the worst out of you.

I have always said that basically, when things go wrong it is the man's fault. He is supposed to be noble, honorable, principled, virtuous, brave, longsuffering, and full of wisdom and patience.

Alas, your husband failed (as all Adams have failed their Eves). The secret to your recovery is in learning not to resent him. It matters not whether he ever becomes the real man you have needed or not. By not resenting him, you will free your soul to receive the love of God. As long as you resent and judge another, you block God's love from flooding your being.

- *31* -

My Wife Asked Me to Move Out –What Should I Do?

This is an issue I hear all the time. In this article I will consider it as if it were written by a husband wondering what to do.

But first, my favorite quote on the matter:

As for his secret to staying married: "My wife tells me that if I ever decide to leave, she is coming with me."

-- Jon Bon Jovi

You go, girl!

Generally, for spiritual reasons, I recommend that you not be the one who initiates the divorce.

If your partner moves out or files for divorce, "it is still a free country," as old the expression goes. But if you make the first move, then you have the guilt of it.

Generally divorce is not a good thing, so initiating it puts the burden of guilt on you. This advice applies to both husband and wife.

There is the situation where the other person is drug addict, criminal, or abusive person. Of course, you have to protect yourself and the children. You might have to get the help of the authorities.

But in this chapter, I'm addressing the more typical situation where both husband and wife are decent, good people.

When both are good people, it is best not to divorce.

It is best to work things out. But if the other person is determined to move out or divorce, let them be the first to make the fateful move. You will then know that you did not initiate it and won't have guilt for it.

Now a special word for men: I cannot advise about any legal issues. Also, every circumstance is different, but I can speak in generalities. For spiritual, emotional, and strategic reasons it is not good for the husband to leave first.

Why is it generally not good for the husband to leave first?

In the mind of the wife, he made the first move and left her. She may have teased him and tempted him to leave first (secretly in her heart of hearts she may have hoped he would not leave her), but, after all, he did not have to leave. He could have stayed. But he did move out.

When he leaves, it means that he walked out. Worse yet, in the eyes of the children, it means that father left them.

Roberto Duran, though one of the greatest boxers in history, will never live down being perceived as a quitter when he said "no mas" in his fight against Sugar Ray Leonard. A dad who leaves has made a bad move. His family will never forget that he moved out on them.

The wife has the advantage now in every respect. She did not leave him. He moved out on her and left the kids.

You see, husband/father has a very special role. He holds a station in life. He holds the office of husband and if there are kids, the office of father.

In the eyes of children, father stands in for God. Can you see why it is so devastating when a father fails?

Husband and father are supposed to be like the George Washington or Moses of the family. He stands for what is right. He cannot have any vices. He must be principled, honorable, wise, patient, long suffering, and kind.

He has to be as steady as the ticking of a grandfather clock in a thunderstorm. If others fail him, he does not fail them. If others become upset, he remains calm and reasonable.

Most dads are a little weak. They say the right things, but say them too weakly.

He should not be there to win a popularity contest. He has to stand for what is right and persist even in the face of rebellion. But he must not be angry. He must always have a twinkle in his eye.

Many men clam up, but are angry and resentful underneath. When they do finally speak up, their message is tainted and ruined by the pent up anger.

Feeling guilty, he remains silent even when something should be said, or he sits on the sidelines while the family goes to ruin.

A man simply can't avoid his duty without harming the family. That is why he must learn to stand for what is right with patience and firmness and kindness.

He has to be there for his wife and children. They need a very special love from him: emotionless agape love. A man cannot have this love if he is selfish or unprincipled. Nor can he have this love for them if he is a womanizer or tries to make his wife into his mother. He must not look for ego support from the world. He must look within and find a bond with what he knows in his heart.

He will then not *need* love. He will *give* love. He must love principle more than anything, even his wife.

But if you think about it for a moment, you will see that this is the man she can trust. She knows he will always be there for her and she knows he will never be unfaithful (because he does not *need* the love of a woman, a drug, or some worldly support). This is the man she can respect and perhaps even love.

Now, gentlemen, most wives are aware of their husband's weaknesses before they get married, but she hopes that he will become the noble knight she needs.

Once within the confines of marriage, the nobly inclined man will become aware of his failing her in some mysterious way.

He will search his heart and out of true concern for her and the children, he will start to see what they need from him. He will learn to be less selfish, and eventually one day, unselfish. He will begin to fail less, and one day not fail at all.

She will see his nobility, his heart felt efforts, and his love of principle. With this man, there is hope.

Of course, there are some women who will not take kindly to his new inner authority, and she will most likely resent him even when he is right. If she is a permanent hater, then she will make his life as miserable as possible. If he remains noble, she will probably go off to find someone else. If this happens, so be it.

But you cannot know what is in your wife's heart until you straighten up and fly right. Only then might your noble love draw forth the good in her.

Many women have been so used and unloved that they cannot imagine or believe that a man can be noble.

She may test him and give him a hard time for years (or decades). If he is tested and not found wanting, he will win her heart. They will become very good friends and live happily ever after.

As I said, most men are weak (or weak and violent). Their weakness literally tempts the wife and kids to rebel. So if you have been weak or selfish, before looking at her wrong, first look at your own. See your part in what has gone wrong and repent of it.

Many wives had a father who was not there for her.

She resented him and went out in the world looking for love. What she got was use and abuse at the hands of boyfriends. Since all men failed her, she expects that he husband will too (though a good woman will hope her husband won't fail her).

Perhaps you can see why the man needs to have the wisdom of Solomon and perfect self control. All men have failed, but that is not an excuse for more failing.

You must find the way to fail less.

I cannot say what to do in any particular circumstance. There are just too many particular situations. But I can speak in general terms.

Generally divorce is not a good thing. Sometimes a separation may be of some help, so that both sides can find themselves and get their bearings, but maybe not.

Please note that my comments are directed to the typical situation where both are good people, not perfect of course, but decent. If your spouse is extremely disturbed, violent or criminal, you will need to protect the children and get professional help and assistance from the authorities.

If there is a divorce, it is best not to begin the process yourself. If your wife divorces you, you will then not be guilty for having begun it.

If you have only been married for a short time, things might be worked out, but if there is not true marriage, then going your separate ways may be best.

But when there are children, everything changes. Now the man is both husband and father.

I recently heard a man tell about his father who he loved deeply. His mom was not a nice lady and she made a lot of trouble. His dad stayed there for the sake of the children and was a good father to them. He suffered for decades, but never hated his wife and never complained. The children loved him dearly.

You see, the children were aware of his suffering. They saw his sacrifice and nobility. And they loved him all the more. It didn't matter what mom did. Father was there for them.

But if he had walked out on her and them, what would be foremost in their minds? Not what mom did, but what he did. He would have quit on them. Thank God he did not.

Dear Sir,

I know that marriage can be a severe test. But just as there can be no courage without danger, so likewise there can be no character without a test of that character. A final word. Sometimes we do the right thing by simply not doing the wrong thing. Someone can tempt you to do something wrong or foolish. Just don't do it and you are safe. Always do what you know is right in your heart. Or don't do the wrong thing.

I've always told men--if you have an argument with your wife--whatever you do, don't walk out. Walking out means something to a woman. Just go sit in the living room and watch television or read a book. Let the storm blow over. You may be surprised to see how safe and secure everyone feels (including your wife) when her naughtiness does not cause you to fail.

- *32* -

Change and Trauma: the Legacy of the Human Race

When we change, we see the changes. And when we do, we either defend them or hide them. Of course, there is a third way, one which I hope to awaken you to so that it might help you change back after you have fallen. This way is the way of mourning our wrong, yearning to be better, realizing we can't change ourselves, and crying out to God, Who answers our prayer.

But first I want to discuss the negative aspect, so you might see what you are doing wrong. The way the human race changed for the worse had to do with an initial fall. Adam went from living forever in Paradise to a shortened life, leading to death, lived in a jungle hell.

Adam began to change from a being who could live perpetually to one who would live on through generation (procreation). One body would die but through reproduction leave a replacement body.

It took Adam a long time to change and die, some 900 years. But for us, the progeny of Adam, we are born already changed. We come into the world as little ego animals. We grow to become big egos in dying bodies. We employ pride to defend, justify, rationalize and excuse our failings.

We might even manage to see our failings as virtues and our falling as rising. That is why society worships compensated people. But their immediate family knows what failures they are.

That is why pseudo scientists tout evolution. If we can believe the lie that we are getting better, then we can excuse death (instead of seeing it as evidence of failure) and accept every behavior as natural because we are just animals.

As we go through life, we add our own particular brand of cultural and personal failings, and these also bring change. Remember—the legacy of the human race and the curse that attends us (unless we find salvation) is change for the worse. And so in each of our failings and fallings, we devolve a little and move closer to death.

There is both a spiritual and a physical aspect. Spiritually we give up a little bit of our innocence and humanity, and we take up the nature of the tempter.

Responding to stress for humans means taking in the stress, incorporating it, and becoming it.

Spiritually, we change in the image of the tempter. The tempter is whoever seduces you to respond emotionally and to cop out (through conformity or rebellion) to the animal way of living. Remember—spiritually, humans either grow nobler, more gracious, more wise, more loving, and more thoughtful, or we grow more base, more hateful, more cunning and vicious.

Change is inevitable. The only question is: will you be able to stand back and admit the truth about your fallen existence, wish to be better but realize that it is not within your power to change yourself for the better. If so, you are on the threshold of returning to the original Light standard and becoming rehumanized.

You see, we are spiritual beings. As spiritual beings, we need love, knowledge, motivation, protection, and something to grow into. And when God is not our overshadowing spirit, then we take our motivation, our knowledge, our support, and image from the temptation to which we have responded.

In fact, you even see this process operating at very basic psychological level. When a person responds to some challenge, he may become a lifelong aficionado, convert and supporter of whatever he or she responded to. One person saw a bird being killed (by another animal) in the forest. He reacted so much to the incident that he became a lifelong bird artist. He devoted his life to birds. One lady saw her aunt die of cancer, and she became a doctor dedicated to fighting cancer.

Another person was an atheist. He was challenged to read the Bible and refute it. But in the process he was converted over and then spent his life as a big evangelist. The little girl seen running from a napalmed village in Viet Nam wanted to become a doctor and eventually became a nurse. Her reaction to the medical treatment converted her.

Emotional conversion is the rule, rather than the exception. How about rock music fans, Elvis fans, or people addicted to playing the slot machines? They have all been converted through an emotional reaction to some event.

It is very sad because those people never become the self they were meant to be. They become the extension of some emotional scene to which they were converted.

Of course, some of life's greatest achievers became devotees of medicine, the arts, science, or public service through emotional conversion. The supporters of college sports, such as alumni sponsors, as well as the donators to charity causes are converts. They give millions of dollars.

So are the alumni that give cars and money to athletes under the table? How about the devotees of radical Islam, of Stalin, Mao or Hitler? How about the crazed environmentalists or proponents of a woman's right to choose to kill her child? How about the Stockholm syndrome, where a person is held and mistreated by terrorists, and then refuses to testify against them?

You see, the terrorists, the seducers, the motivators, and culture in general have a lot going for them. All they have to do is emotionally shock people, and a large percentage will be converted over to the experience, whether it be a positive one or a negative one. Even the positive ones (where someone is challenge to respond emotionally to serve some "good" cause) are really negative. The convert may serve well, but it is not as a free spirit. The convert has literally lost his own identity.

As a great man once said, trauma is imprinted on the psyche. This is true for both humans and animals.

Moreover, this is both genetic/species wide (in other words inherited), and also specific to a particular animal or person who encounters a trauma in his life.

First let's look at a couple of species wide inherited imprinting. Somehow a small bird recognizes the hovering shape of a hawk overhead. Despite the fact that that particular bird has never encountered a hawk.

It is inherited from some long distant trauma to the race of these birds.

When confronted with danger, a certain African beetle joins with hundred of its fellow beetles to form the shape of a flower (in order to fool the predator into thinking the beetles are a flower). The amazing thing is that this particular flower has been extinct for hundreds of years! Yet, the beetles still form this shape. This response is somehow ingrained and perpetuated from generation to generation.

When it comes to humans, a trauma is imprinted on the psyche of the human race. In the Garden of Eden, Adam disobeyed God and his eyes were opened. In a sense, his inner eye was closed and his external eyes were opened to know in a new (and lower way).

In the trauma, the first thing he saw was Eve, the woman. And her image was imprinted on his psyche.

To this day, the image of woman is imprinted on the male's psyche. Men inherently find women fascinating and scary, exciting and threatening. And, of course, this inherent fascination is overlaid by the particular women the boy and man encounter.

The seductiveness or indomitable presence and distraction of his own mother is often the biggest traumatic influence in his life.

The woman's form, her speech, her words, her distractive presence, and her food all combine to imprint the boy's psyche with an experience and seductive trauma he never gets beyond. Whether he loves her or hates her, or a combination of both, he is a creature of trauma and his choices in later life will often be women who resemble his unloved, seductive and confusing mom.

The thing about trauma is that although it might, and often is, at first repulsive, it then becomes a fascination and attractive.

You see, trauma has two sides to it. The extreme reaction causes a shift from repulsion to attraction (and sometimes back again). Pavlov discovered this. For the traumatized person or animal, at a certain stage, hate turns to love, repulsion to attraction, dislike to like. This reversal is just prior to the ultimate reaction which is a complete wiping away of prior behavioral patterns and a complete reprogramming.

It appears that for humans, we have an inherited remembrance of the trauma in as much as the woman, the spoken word, the lie, food, and even evil itself are inherently fascinating.

So, of course, cagey manipulators of all stripes take advantage of our inherent fascination with woman, food, words, lies, and naughtiness to capture our attention and draw us into having power over us.

Remember that in trauma, there is at first a spreading protective inhibition over the conscious mind. This self protective mechanism serves the purpose of protecting the brain from damage. But it also serves the purpose of the one who knows how to use trauma to gain control over us. In the presence of our seducer or tyrant, we become putty in their hands. We experience then love and hate them or whoever or whatever they direct our love/hate to, and we eventually become reprogrammable.

Bear in mind that the original trauma in the Garden makes certain circumstances inherently fascinating. We recognize something about the scene and are virtually drawn to it to test the waters or find out what is all about and why it is so fascinating.

Another example is the ubiquitous human propensity to seek a high, through drug taking or other means.

What is the high but the same thing Adam sought? He sought to be like a god apart from God. And so through our music, our rituals, and our drugs we seek

262

to feel good like God. And when our drug induced highs lead to debilitation, we then seek peace apart from God using drugs, false meditations, or other techniques to become oblivious to conscience and to enjoy a false peace apart from God.

Getting back to the theme of this chapter, the inherent fascination with the high is our inherited fascination and attraction to that ancient trauma producing drug taking in the Garden of Eden.

Incidentally, at a more subtle level, the original temptation object was food. And to this very day, it is food that ferrets us away from reality to a food induced high. We celebrate with food and we console ourselves with food. The eating of food (or food-like drugs, alcohol, marijuana, and nicotine) to induce an altered state of consciousness is a universal human propensity.

Again, our fascination and fixation on food and drugs is evidence of an original trauma.

Another fascination we have is with death. We can't help but gawk and rubber neck at any accident on the road. We fear death, but we are also fascinated by it.

Death was part of the trauma in the Garden. Death is the evidence of failing, just as sex is the evidence of our failing. Sex leads to the life that leads to death. Sex and death are fascinating. It is not by accident that the French call the sex climax *la petite mort* (the little death).

Finally, I want to mention women's fascination with failing men. The human race sprang into existence because of the trauma of Adam's failing. He lost paradise. His dereliction and blame of his wife ushered in a world of intrigue, fighting and suffering.

The trauma of her man failing, the loss of paradise, and the blame he placed on her all traumatized her and sensitized her. The proof of the original trauma in the Garden is in virtually every woman today. She cannot help but notice and judge men's failures and judge them for it. She loathes weak and failing men on the one hand, but can't help but be fascinated by them on the other. She is sensitive to the blame, and often blames herself when things go wrong. Then she serves her failing man out of guilt (for having judged and hated him). And her service only supports what is wrong with him, making him worse.

So you see, men and women are locked into fascination, trauma, love and hate—an inherited sensitivity, fascination, fear and attraction to each other.

All of which is inherited (and then reinforced throughout life) from an initial trauma at the inception of the human race.

Each partner reinforces the other's role in the tragic drama. And because their interaction is trauma based, each emotional incident imprints something of the other on each.

A traumatic situation is one that the organism or person must adapt to. It is a stress and it leaves an imprinted image behind. The organism has to draw upon energy to adapt (conform, rebel, fight or flight) and reach some sort of accommodation with the sustaining stress. Some stresses, like a little infection in a cut, can be overcome through the bodily responses.

The body wins, the germs lose. And the body has a memory of how to fight the germ.

Other stresses are constant and for want of strength or because of their very nature, become chronic. The body must adapt to them, but this adaptation uses up energy.

Now in the case of the man and woman. The woman is the stress for the man. Ideally, he should overcome her naughtiness and temptation with love and wisdom.

And when he wins, they both win. He draws forth inner wisdom and love. And she, responding to the love and wisdom coming through him, is won over to also respect and serve that good.

The man is overcome by the stress of the Spirit of Love and Understanding which comes from God by way of conscience. Submitting to conscience and then learning to serve God, this man now becomes a stress to others. But this time he is a good stress--his honesty and persistent patience stress others to become better.

The temporarily lost or naughty are imprinted by the memory of the good they encounter in him, to which they one day respond and conform out of a free will choice. (The permanently bad are stressed and imprinted by the truth that shines through the good person. And they then carry out a losing resentful battle against the spirit of truth which destroys them in the end).

In this happy scenario, the woman whose husband has found an inner bond with the Creator, can just let her hair down and be herself. Her husband will have the wisdom and understanding with which to deal with her temptation. When they were married, he undoubtedly married her for the temptation in her. But now that he is wiser, he can now love her for herself not for the temptation.

She will, of course, try him. He will be sorely tested by her, perhaps for months, years or even decades. She will test him to see if his love is true. If he falls, she gets an unhealthy feeling of judgment and superiority (but yet, if she is a decent woman, part of her will be disappointed and sad). But if he is persistently patient and wise, the goodly woman will come to respect and then to love the good that comes through him and gently conquers her dark side. Her love of the good in him is the same as a love and respect for the Creator.

So it is a win-win situation. When he wins (when reason overcomes emotion, when principle overcomes naughtiness), they both win. Good triumphs over temptation.

He becomes the knight in shining armor. She becomes the beautiful graceful woman (instead of a teasing nag). The kids see the goodness operating and they relate to it and respect it.

But now let's look at what usually happens. The man marries the woman who supports his ego. Her support makes him more selfish, more beastly, or more ambitious. He becomes addicted to and dependent on her support. I must say at this point that I am not blaming her.

It is his fault. He is the one who is misusing her love. She can't help but support his ego. Why? First of all, in his fallen egotistical condition, he is basically a user. He uses everything to support his ego, his pride, and his beastly nature. Secondly, it is a woman's nature to be a helpmate to her husband. If he is good, then she is helping the good. But if he is prideful, then she ends up serving his pride.

If she were to withdraw her support, he would become enraged and demanding of her support. But when she gives it he becomes worse.

In response to the support, some men become wimpy. She becomes the dominant power, and he walks around on egg shells to curry and get her support.

Pity the poor woman. She gave her love, only to find that it makes her husband a bigger beast or a bigger wimp. His wrong and his weakness temp her to nag him—to try to make him into a man. But he only becomes more dependent on her nagging to function (or more rebellious to it).

His weakness and failing tempt the family to hold him in contempt. If he is a wimp they walk all over him. If he is an angry brute, they fear, loathe, and judge him for his wrong. Soon the whole family is in rebellion against the wrong dad.

In some families, dad becomes a permanent wimp. Mom is in charge. She rules the house. She may pretend that he is in charge, but she only lets him be in charge (she is the real source of power).

He might become ambitious, becoming married to his work or to money. She tolerates or encourages this situation because of the power it gives her, and the perks she gets from the money he makes.

Instead of looking at himself when things go wrong, he blames her. Because of his craving for ego support, he may look for it from another woman, from the bottle, from peers, or from work. He may become a drunk or a successful businessman. He uses his success to support his ego, and he becomes a success, but a success who is an empty shell.

The successful empty shell finds friends, organizations, support groups, or religions that support him in his egotistical shallow wrong. The drunk or drug addict finds drugs and low life colleagues to support him. There are even religious groups that will accept him just as he is.

I write this to awaken the potential child of the light, man or woman, to see the truth about why men and women are always fighting and making each other unhappy. I write in the hope that awakening to truth, the seeker may see that we are all born into this fallen system. That we all have an ego nature that demands support, and thereby we become more wrong. As we become more wrong, we tend to blame others. However, if the seeker can see the truth, he or she may be able to forgive by dropping grudges.

When we let go of our resentments against dad, mom, boyfriend, husband, wife, we will stop being stressed emotionally and stop having the ones we resent as our environment to which we must adapt.

What Paul calls the old man, the Adamic man (or woman) is the fallen reactive, emotional, adapting, and deteriorating self. When the soul learns to stand back and draw nearer to the inner light, it takes a new imprint—that of a Godly origin. And the self that will develop over time, lots of time, is the growing child of God.

Every time you are patient, every time you overlook (without judgment), every time you deny your (faulty) self the pleasure of anger/resentment, you will be fortified in the spirit. Your character develops to the extent that you don't react, don't resent, and don't take advantage. Every moment in which you withhold judgment and remain patient permits your new character to grow. Do you see the Divine paradox? The less you do (in terms of resenting, getting angry, compensating, and huffing and puffing), the more happens.

Paul said: "I die daily." In other words, the old self dies as it is denied its kicks. The new self flowers. Christ said that we are to take up our cross and deny ourselves. In other words, we are to willingly, as a free will sacrifice, give up the ego building and sustaining indulgences in resentment, irritation, excitement, and ambitious activity.

We love by not hating. We grow by not compensating. We grow in spiritual riches by not indulging the flesh.

This can only be done, of course, with God's grace. And it won't happen overnight. It takes time, lots of time. Yet, this long process begins in the twinkling of an eye.

When the soul receives the touch of God, the person is raised in awareness enough to see the need to meditate and the need for patience. For the first time, the person will be able to meditate properly, and with each passing day, will receive delicate insights. These insights mostly reveal error. And seeing the error, the misbelief, the wrong attitude (that the person could not see before), the individual is able to step back and deal with the error properly.

- 33 -

A Mother's Lament - My Son Doesn't Listen to Me

How many times have I heard moms say this? Usually it involves a preteen or teenage son. Often dad is not there, perhaps because of divorce. Mom is left alone with the kids.

I hope this chapter will shed some light on the subject so that both sons and moms can understand each other better—and love and not resent each other. I will address single and divorced moms, though my advice should also prove enlightening for any mom or parent to be.

First of all, I understand that it is difficult to raise a child when you are a single mom. I have compassion for your situation. I wish your husband were there for you. But he is not. So I have to deal with the present situation, not what we would like it to be.

There is an old expression: the boy is father to the man. And in keeping with this truism, a boy wants to someday be a man.

A boy wants to begin doing the things a man can do. He wants to be competent and good at something. He wants to be strong and courageous. He wants to know how to do things and fix things. He wants to be worthy of respect. He wants to one day be a good provider. He wants to be a man.

It is tough if dad is not there. It helps if there are role models around: teachers, neighbors, coaches, a good older brother, uncle, or grandpa.

But no matter how many or few role models there are around, a boy needs opportunities to be a man (albeit a young man).

Now, it takes a very wise and perceptive mom to be cognizant of the above and to defer a little and give him a chance to lead.

Many ladies do not realize what a force they are. It is easy to be bossy. It is easy for a mom, being older and being far more verbally skilled, to always be right. It is easy to always win the argument with your child. It is easy to accuse and berate.

It even happens that a mom will unconsciously resent her son because he is a male (like other men she has resented) and who reminds her of them by the mere fact that he is a male.

Having experienced violence or use at the hands of a man, it is tempting to put down her son. I'm sorry to have to say this. But it does happen and has to be mentioned.

Even the best of parents has a tendency to become a bit bossy and authoritarian at times. When we were kids we were bossed around. It feels good to turn around and do it to someone else. And yes, big brothers, big sisters, baby sitters, and aunts can be and often are bossy too.

Mom gets used to issuing orders and commands. Being directive (as long as it is with kindness) is appropriate for little kids, who need direction. But when kids get older, delegation is usually more appropriate.

When an older boy or girl is just told what to do, there is no space for self direction. But self direction and the development of independence, self motivation, and responsibility are what older kids need.

Perhaps you can have some sympathy for the plight of the boy. Surrounded by mostly women authorities, and being bossed around, he hardly has a chance to be a man.

A wise mom (graced with high self esteem and love) will sometimes let her son lead. Remember the old fashioned style of dancing (such as ball room or square dancing)? The man leads. If mom occasionally lets her older son lead when it comes to a few decisions around the home, it is actually a gracious and noble thing.

If a boy has a chance to be the man of the family-- serving as big brother to siblings, watching out for them, fixing things, and even sharing in decision making—you would be surprised how many such young men will rise to the occasion.

It takes wisdom, grace and a lot of love to stand back and let the young man be protective and helpful. But it must not be too obvious. I love the old television shows (such as *Andy of Mayberry, Leave It to Beaver,* or *Father Knows Best*) because they show how a parent can be vigilant without being intrusive.

I'm especially fond of the television series *The Big Valley,* where the main character (played by Barbara Stanwyck) is the matriarch of a powerful California ranch family. She shows how to be strong but not pushy, and both competent and gracious. Because she was not over-bearing, her kids were strong and had self esteem too.

It is amazing how much wisdom was written into these old television shows. For example, they often portray a story where the parents are secretly watching what one of the children is doing, but pretending not to see.

They stay in the shadows--vigilant and observant, ready to help out or even take charge if necessary--but hoping the child will do what is right on her own..

And even if the child makes a mistake (the parents watch to make sure that nothing really bad happens), it is a learning experience. The child was allowed to handle it himself (though the parents were quietly on guard). Another win-win is when the child sees for himself that he is in over his head and comes to the parents for advice.

There is even a passage in the Bible where it says that Mary watched her son from the distance and held things in her heart. Not everything has to be said. Some things are guarded in the heart. Nor does everything need to be said right away. People need a little space to discover for themselves.

Finally, here is one of my favorite helpful hints for parents and especially moms (since most single parent homes are headed by moms). I heard one of America's top family experts casually state this gem as an aside.

When I heard it, I immediately knew it was right and have never forgotten it.

He said this to parents, and especially parents of teenagers: "Don't be so confrontational."

When a parent disproves of something that a child has done, there is a tendency to get right in his face.

Not only is this painful to watch and even more painful to be on the receiving end of, it also tempts the child to become angry, and then either secretly hostile or to become a wimp.

Give them some space. Remember the cute song "Talk to the Animals" from the movie Dr. Doolittle?

Talk to the family pet, talk to the pictures on the wall, talk to the stuffed animals on the shelf. Tell them what is going on. Say it so that your child can overhear what you are saying to the stuffed teddy bear on the shelf.

Say to the teddy bear: "I don't know what to do. I've got company coming in half an hour, but John (the 12 year old son in question) says he has to go visit Joey next door. I need someone to help me vacuum the living room. Jane is at ballet. I have to prepare food. John is going next door. Oh, what am I going to do?"

You would be surprised how many times, after a few minutes go by, John, (who overheard your conversation with the bear), will suddenly appear and say: "Mom, I heard you tell Bear about your dilemma. I gave it some thought, and I decided I better call Joey and tell him I can't come over because I've got to help my mom!"

He realized it himself, grew in character, and will feel good about himself--all because you gave him the space to see it for himself.

In conclusion, boys need opportunities for work, for competition, and for sports. A boy needs to have something that he feels competent doing. If possible the activities should be real: not looking at pictures of hiking, but hiking; not just watching a movie about swimming, but really swimming.

Most importantly, he needs opportunities to lead and make decisions. What better place to learn than at home under the wise and gentle tutelage of his parent?

- 34 -

Advice to Divorced Moms

First of all, I must say again what I have said many times before. Kids generally don't like divorce. They love to see mommy and daddy together, loving each other forever. God intended it that way.

Kids are very perceptive and being closer to God, see reality. They can basically see something wrong with divorce. It affects them deeply. It means that something is profoundly wrong and out of order. It is a betrayal. It makes them feel insecure.

I know there are spouses who are drug dealers, gang members, violent or abusive. I understand that in such circumstances, separation and divorce is often absolutely necessary for self-protection and protection of the kids. If your spouse is a violent criminal and you are afraid, get help from the authorities. Use the full force of the law to protect your children and yourself.

If you are in danger, get help.

But in this chapter I would like to focus on the more typical situation where both mom and dad, or husband and wife, are good people. It is sad to see a divorce over little misunderstandings and selfishness when both partners are good people. If I can help in some miniscule way in preventing a divorce and helping two good people stay together and work things out—I am happy.

If a divorce has happened, then we have to deal with what is. Before going any further, let me just go ahead and give you my opinion of what would be really nice (though it rarely happens) if a divorce has already happened.

It would be nice if both mom and dad remain unmarried. Both do a lot of soul searching and begin to realize that each was basically selfish, he in his way and she in her way. Both become more forgiving and drop their resentments against the other.

He sees that she is just a lady. And she sees that he is just a man. Each had wanted perfection; each was resentful over not getting some need met; each was resentful. Now both have matured and are more forgiving.

He realizes that he has to be a man, shoulder the responsibility for what went wrong, and learn to be more fatherly. He sees that he was weak, that he was a selfish user, and that he was not committed to principle.

She sees that she had become moody and resentful, wallowing in judgment of his weaknesses and failings.

Her catering to him may have been sneaky and dishonest—it was out of guilt for the resentment, not out of love. She sees that she resented him because he was like her dad or all men. She sees that she wanted to be his god and motivate and change him. Now she sees that he did have some good qualities, but she never gave him the space to find himself.

276

After a series of profound realizations, both are sobered and chastened. Both get back together, now more mature.

But as I said, this is rare. Mostly one or both sides continue to blame the other. Sometimes one or both claim to have forgiven, and even say that they are now good "friends" with the other. But there has to be something wrong here, because if they are such good friends, why not make good their original commitment?

Mostly, the friendly talk is face saving. No one wants to be perceived as bitter and hurt. So both cavalierly say that all is fine.

Then there is the pitiful situation where both get back together, but it's more of a codependency thing. He says he's sorry for gambling/cheating on her. Or whatever. And she accepts him back. But nothing has changed. He is still weak and immature (or violent), and she resents him and then serves him out of guilt.

Now that we have that out of the way, let's address the most likely present circumstances.

Here is the key principle. It is very important that the kids not be taught or encouraged to hate their father.

This does not mean that you have to like your ex husband. Nor does it mean that any or all of the kids have to like their dad. It does not mean that if he did some wrong things, that you have to pretend that he didn't or say that it is okay.

The secret to life is to see discern reality without judgment. To see error, clearly and without distortion, but not to hate or resent others. That way, our soul remains safe. We are not penetrated by the wrong or victimized by it. We are free to leave the past behind and enter a bright future with no baggage.

But when we resent another, it leaves a scar and causes trauma. I'm sure you have heard the old expression: it's not so much what happens to you as how you react to it."

Never is this truer than when it comes to resentment and hatred. Kids are resilient. They can survive arguments. They can survive a divorce. They can survive hard times. But as long as they harbor resentment and judgment, they cannot move forward without being harmed and then taking this baggage into the future and ruining their own life and their relationships.

It is a basic spiritual law: hate your parents and hurt your kids. I did not make this up. It comes from a master counselor with 50 years experience. I repeat it here because it is true.

Therefore, don't overtly or covertly encourage your child to hate his or her dad. If you do, and the child does hate his or her father, this will harm the child; and someday when they realize that your influence overtly or subtly contributed to their hate; they will be tempted to hate you too.

It will be much easier to not subtly influence your kids to hate (since they are bonded to you and pick up you feelings), if you yourself drop your resentments against your ex husband.

Remember, forgiving does not mean pretending everything is alright or liking what another did.

Forgiving does not mean having to be friends or even having anything to do with another. It just means dropping resentment. It means dropping grudges. It means letting go of hostility.

Forgiving really has much less to do with the other person than it does your inner relationship with conscience. When the inner light of conscience repents you of your resentments, you have a change of attitude.

Your soul is unburdened, and you are reconciled to the God of conscience. Thus you can forgive someone who is a thousand miles away or long dead and buried.

As far as your kids go, let me mention that the office of fatherhood is very important. Father has a special role: he represents God in the eyes of a child. When dad fails, it is a big deal.

But, the child will be okay if he does not resent his or her dad.

It is also a spiritual law that hatred of father puts up a road block between the person and God.

Another way of saying it is: you cannot love your Heavenly Father if you hate your earthly father.

A human is meant to eventually find the God of conscience. This occurs later in life, often during the second half of life when a person begins to yearn for truth. Resentment of father blocks this from happening (until it is seen and let go of).

Chances are—you probably have some issues with your dad. Chances are he wasn't there for you. You resented him and went out in the world looking for love. What you found was someone like your dad.

Hopefully you would like your kids to be free to live a happy and productive life without issues and hang ups.

Their best chance, in fact their only chance, is if they don't resent their parents.

Because your kids are human beings, they will have to make their own choices. Undoubtedly your kids do resent their dad. You cannot make them not resent him—just don't encourage it. Talk to them in general terms about the importance of forgiveness. Don't manipulate them for affection. Admit freely your own errors. But don't look for sympathy.

Let them see reality. Don't force them to see you as wonderful. Don't pretend. Don't blame.

Hold your head up high, and move forward with your life. Keep your fears and worries to yourself. Go about your business, and watch out for emotion-charged atmospheres. No child likes seeing his mom a basket case. Kids like to see their parent calm and getting better, not worse.

Finally, I must address the topic of dating and remarrying. Again I must say that kids generally do not like a strange man coming around. Most kids are wary.

They often view a stranger as trying to take dad's place.

I must say that it is best to be very, very cautious about dating. What kind of a man wants to immediately horn in on another family and come between a man and wife and any chance of reconciliation?

As I said: best to remain chaste. If you have a male friend, let him be a true platonic friend. Do not force your kids to like some new "friend." Do not force them to respect him.

Kids are perceptive. Sometimes a child will see a dark side to someone that you can't see.

The number one rule: protect your kids.

If possible, forget about men and dating for four or five years. Don't make it an issue. Spend time with your kids, perhaps becoming established in business, and sorting things out.

Proceed with caution. It can happen that the first husband was a loser. The wife continues on after the divorce with dignity, living a decent and chaste life. She lets go of her grudges against men, and becomes well established, perhaps a successful businesswoman.

Moreover, she discovers what it was about herself that made her the type of woman that got involved with that type of man.

Now having matured and changed, she becomes the type of woman who will attract a decent man.

With time, a gentleman with a noble heart does enter her life.

After a long period of platonic acquaintanceship and getting to know him very well, and after a lengthy chaste friendship, she sees that he is interested in her as a person, not an object of use. Then there can be a true marriage of two noble people.

If there are kids--the virtue, the nobility, the chasteness, and the fatherly quality of this man will not tempt them to judge or resent him. With time they may come to respect or even love him.

In the meantime, hold your head up high, and learn to grow in grace.

- *35* -

What is the Number One Cause of Divorce?

Are you stressed out? Have you noticed that when you are resentful, you become more sensitive to life's little issues? When you are stressed at work, do you come home and easily lose patience with your kids? Do you come home and resent your husband over some little things that he does?

Do you get angry at slow traffic or slow grocery lines? Would terms like "exasperated, nervous, irritated, or impatient" describe you?

If so, you are probably over-reacting. And the worst reaction of all is that of resentment. It sets you up for becoming increasingly sensitive to what you might otherwise take in stride.

I know, times are tough. The problem is that most of us do not know how to pay attention without becoming upset by what we see. Early in life, we encountered unfairness and were dragged into bad situations, and we became upset. Trouble is: now we do not know how to deal with injustice or mean people without being upset.

Worse yet, we do not even know how to observe other people's little imperfections without judging or resenting them. Early in life, someone was unfair with us, and we got upset. Someone teased us and we got upset. We were conditioned to become upset. And not knowing how not to be upset, we became resentful and judgmental toward others.

But what then happened is that we learned to resent and judge others as a compensation for having been on the receiving end of injustice to which we copped out. We could hate someone for their wrong, and secretly gloat in a sense of superiority.

Admittedly it is hard when we were a child to speak up to a towering parent or teacher, but when possible it is much better to have the courage to speak up over injustice with what reason and composure we can muster than to remain silent and harbor secret hostility and resentment.

When we became adults, we continued to have the habit of becoming upset and saying nothing, but secretly judging. So when our spouse turned out to be less than perfect, we began to secretly judge him. When he would not bow to our will or when we were disappointed by him, we reveled in judgment and hurt feelings.

And when someone smaller than you came along, like your kids for instance, it felt good to dump on them when they spilled some milk or did not pay attention.

Now the shoe was on the other foot. As a child you were on the receiving end of some authority's wrath and impatience. Now, as an adult you may relieve yourself by taking it out on your kids. But this is totally unfair.

I can honestly tell you that the number one reason for marriage break ups and relationship problems is resentment.

I know--most of us do not really want to be mean or impatient. We do not really want to judge our husband or yell at our kids. But we do not know how to stop ourselves. We get out of control, and then either blow up or else suppress and get a headache or tummy ache.

Some people even turn to pills or alcohol to try to control their upset. Others turn their judgment on themselves. In short, they end up hating themselves when they see that they have become just like those that were mean to them when they were a child.

Here at the Center for Common Sense Counseling we help people learn to stop over-reacting. We teach them about giving up resentment and about being patient with others. We help people to see that it is resentment that destabilizes them and makes them easily upset.

And it is resentment that keeps reinforcing the upset.

Being upset is a way of life for us. It supports our ego. If we did not have something to be upset over, we would become bored and would not even have motivation to do anything!

Most of us are motivated by upset, irritation, or pressure. We even use upset as a spur to activity. We then use the energy of resentment and anger to get a lot done.

After we have been upset, and then fatigued and tense, we use it as an excuse to "unwind." We look forward to our after-work drink, our marijuana, pleasure or party. We become thirstier and hungrier when we are upset. Pleasure feels better when it takes away tension and pain.

But if you were not upset, nervous, or tense in the first place, you would not need relief in the second place. Unnecessary pleasure or releases would feel unnatural. Billions of dollars a year a made on people's needs for pills, booze, drugs, vacations, and diversions.

It's big business. Not to mention all the doctor bills and hospital bills when our excessive upsets and unnatural forms of relief catch up to us physically. Now you know: for most people, being upset, nervous irritated and angry, after which they seek pleasure and relief, is the only life they know.

But I assure you: there is a way of living without being upset, which is full of joy and true purpose. It begins when you learn how to not resent and be impatient with others.

The second reason why we are upset all the time is this: most of us think we have a right to be upset. We think we have the right to judge and the right to resent.

Upset adds an edge to our judgment and resentment. When you resent someone in line ahead of you for being slow, you can then "feel" that judgment as irritation. When your kids want something when you are trying to "unwind" after work, you resent their demands, become impatient, and then feel the resentment.

When your husband does not meet your needs, you can secretly resent him and judge his weaknesses. You can feel the upset (or the headache), and then get another round of ego boost by resenting him for "causing" your discomfort. Then your ego can get yet another ego high by feeling like a martyr, giving your service to an unappreciative good-for-nothing husband.

Since we think we have a right to resent and judge, and since we use our upset for our ego and for intensification of pleasure, most of us do not want to give it up. Our whole life is built on resentment and upset.

Yes, you have the right to resent, but is that really the human and compassionate way of living? How do you feel when others exercise their right to be angry and resentful toward you?

For some of us, it is only when our upsets lead to health problems, headaches, ulcers, ruined relationships, or addictions, that we are stopped short in our tracks long enough to see the need to give it up our "right" to resent.

Some people just will not give up what is killing them. They go on reveling in irritations and secret hostility, and then pay the piper. But there are some, and perhaps you are one of them, who do not like the way they are.

They do not like their secret judgments. They see their anger and do not like it. They yearn to be kind and patient. They yearn to live the good life. But after years of over-reacting, they do not know how to stop reacting and being upset.

That is where someone like me can help. I know what you need. You need two things. First, how to be still.

That is what our stillness meditation is for. It teaches you how to become still and re-find your center of dignity. When you re-find your own center of dignity, you will be able to flow from within; instead of reacting to externals and becoming upset.

Secondly, you need some basic training about life. You probably learned to become upset and emotional over things when you were a child. Chances are -- your mother was emotional and you picked it up from her.

Most likely your dad was weak or a nonfactor. Dads are supposed to represent calmness and self control, and demonstrate how to live life with patience and courage without suppressing on the one hand or being angry on the other.

Few people nowadays are there to stand for calmness and composure. Mostly everyone encourages us to get excited, party, be ambitious, yell at sports events, and so on. Maybe you had good parents, grandparents, a good teacher, coach, or minister who talked about self control, forgiveness, and taking things in stride. But you did not listen.

Now years later, and suffering from your excesses, you are ready to listen. Just trying to deal with the symptoms of resentment is not enough, you must learn how to nip it in the bud before it has a chance to fester and ruin your marriage.

- 36 -

My Wife Cheated on Me – Now What?

This question is coming up more and more. I am very sorry to hear this. It is much more common nowadays than before. Many, if not most, women are now in the workforce. There are a lot of temptations out there.

Also, many people have a different view of marriage today than people did years ago. Today we have been shown on television, movies, and through music, and we have even been taught and counseled that marriage is about having our needs met.

Actually, marriage is a framework for raising a family and in which to learn how not to be selfish.

I've written some articles and posts about the issue of unfaithful husbands. So I guess it's time to talk to men about the issue of unfaithful wives. I've been talking to people about relationships for over 20 years on the radio, written a couple of books and more than a few articles and blog posts, and my wife and I just celebrated our silver wedding anniversary, so I've got as much right as the next guy to write about this topic.

So here is my response. First the short answer. (Some of this material was already introduced in a previous chapter, but it is so important I am re-iterating it here).

Some busy men will not have time to read the whole book. They want an answer to the pressing infidelity issue. So here it is.

If you just found out, stay calm. Do not do anything rash. Go about your business, do your duty, go to work, be there for your kids. You've heard the old expression "stand back and count to ten." Well, stand back and maybe let a few weeks go by. As time passes the initial anger will diminish. Watch out for resentment. Let reason rule.

It takes a real man to stay the course and respond with calm reason instead of anger.

There is value in being able to talk it out. Most communities have government, nonprofit, church, or volunteer organizations focusing on men's issues, marriage or anger management. Avail yourself of any that are helpful. There are also resources available on the internet.

Long term you don't want to become dependent on external support, but right now reading, talking it out, and getting good feedback from someone knowledgeable with understanding are very helpful.

If it happened a few months or years ago, and it is still sticking in your craw, it means that you are still resentful. Watch out for resentment. Stand back and when you see it rising, observe it from the neutral zone and let it pass.

Now the longer answer.

The advice I have given to women in this circumstance (where a husband has been unfaithful) is just as fitting for men. Basically, the woman has to deal with resentment and judgment. If she can let go of these, then she will be spiritually and emotionally safe.

It is resentment that hurts us more than what the other person did to us.

Resentment ruins everything. But if you can let go of the resentment, you will be okay. Moreover, when the mind is clear and not clouded with resentment and bitterness, you will be able to see what is reasonable and wise to do. Remember, resentment robs us of joy and many other things.

I cannot overemphasize the importance of letting go of resentment.

In circumstances of an unfaithful spouse, the woman's main spiritual issues are letting go of resentment and judgment. The man faces a much bigger challenge because of what husband and father represent.

You see, husband or father has a very special role. He holds a station in life. He holds the office of husband and if there are kids, the office of father.

In the eyes of children, father stands in for God. Can you see why it is so devastating when a father fails?

Husband or father is supposed to be like the George Washington or Moses of the family. He stands for what is right. He cannot have any vices. He must be principled, honorable, wise, patient, long suffering, and kind.

He has to be as steady as the ticking of a grandfather clock in a thunderstorm. If others become upset, he remains calm and reasonable. If others fail him, he does not fail them.

Most dads are a little weak. They say the right things, but say them too weakly. He must not be there to win a popularity contest. He has to stand for what is right and persist even in the face of rebellion. But he must not be angry. He must always have a twinkle in his eye.

Many men clam up, but are angry and resentful underneath. When they do finally speak up, their message is tainted and ruined by the pent up anger.

Feeling guilty, he may clam up again or sit on the sidelines while the family goes to ruin.

A man simply cannot avoid his duty without harming the family. That is why he must learn to stand for what is right with patience and firmness and kindness.

He has to be there for his wife and children. They need a very special love from him: emotionless agape love. A man cannot have this love if he is selfish or unprincipled. Nor can he have this love for them if he is a womanizer or tries to make his wife into his mother. He must not look for ego support from the world. He must look within and find a bond with what he knows in his heart.

He will then not need love. He will give love. He must love principle more than anything, even his wife.

However if you think about it for a moment, you will see that this is the man she can trust. She knows he will always be there for her and she knows he will never be unfaithful (because he does not need the love of a woman, a drug, or some worldly support). This is the man she can respect and perhaps even love.

Now, gentlemen, most wives are aware of their husband's weaknesses before they get married, but she hopes that he will become the noble knight she needs.

Once within the confines of marriage, the nobly inclined man will become aware of his failing her in some mysterious way.

He will search his heart and out of true love for her and the children, he will see what they need from him.

He will learn to be less selfish, and eventually one day, unselfish. He will begin to fail less, and one day not fail at all.

She will see his nobility, his heart felt efforts, and his love of principle. With this man, there is hope.

Of course, there are some women who will not take kindly to his new inner authority, and she will most likely resent him even when he is right. If she is a permanent hater, then she will make his life as miserable as possible. If he remains noble, she will probably go off to find someone else. If this happens, so be it.

Before you jump to any conclusions, let me say this: you cannot know what is in your wife's heart until you straighten up and fly right. First you must become right.

Only then might your noble love draw forth the good in her.

Many women have been so used and unloved that they cannot imagine or believe that a man can be noble.

She may test him and give him a hard time for years (or decades). If he is tested and not found wanting, he will win her heart. They will become very good friends and live happily ever after.

As I said, most men are weak (or weak and violent).

Their weakness literally tempts the wife and kids to rebel. So if you have been weak or selfish, before looking at other's wrong, first look at your own. See your part in what has gone wrong and repent of it.

Many wives had a father who was not there for her. She resented him and went out in the world looking for love. What she got was use and abuse at the hands of boyfriends. Since all men failed her, she expects that her husband will too (though a good woman will hope her husband won't fail her).

Perhaps you can see why the man needs to have the wisdom of Solomon and perfect self control. All men have failed, but that is not an excuse for more failing.

You must find the way to fail less. I cannot say what to do in any particular circumstance. There are just too many particular situations. But I can speak in general terms.

Generally divorce is not a good thing. Sometimes a separation may be of some help, so that both sides can find themselves and get their bearings, but maybe not.

Please note that my comments are directed to the typical situation where both are good people--not perfect of course, but decent. If your spouse is extremely disturbed, violent or criminal, you will need to protect the children and get professional help and assistance from the authorities.

If there is a divorce, it is best not to begin the process yourself. If your wife divorces you, you will then not be guilty for having begun it.

If you have only been married for a short time, things might be worked out, but if there is not true marriage, then going your separate ways may be best.

But when there are children, everything changes. Now the man is both husband and father.

I recently heard a man tell about his father who he loved deeply. His mom was not a nice lady and she made a lot of trouble. He stayed there for the children and was a good father to them. He suffered for decades, but never hated his wife and never complained. The children loved him dearly.

You see, the children were aware of his suffering. They saw his sacrifice and nobility. And they loved him all the more. It didn't matter what mom did. Father was there for them.

But if he had walked out on her and them, what would be foremost in their minds would not be what mom did, but what he did. He quit on them.

Dear Sir, I know that infidelity is a severe test. But just as there can be no courage without danger, so likewise there can be no character without a test of that character. A final word. Sometimes we do the right thing by simply not doing the wrong thing. Someone can tempt you to do something wrong or foolish. Just don't do it and you are safe. Always do what you know is right in your heart.

- 37 -

Finding the Best Marriage Advice – Trust Your God Given Instincts

It is obvious that many people have lost their way. This is especially obvious when it comes to marriages.

Look into many families and you will find misunderstanding, resentment, suppressed anger, and hurt feelings. Husbands and wives argue. Parents and kids yell at each other. Communication is poor or nonexistent. Even worse, families are breaking up and divorces are rampant.

It is clear that people need the right kind of guidance. But if I may be so bold as to say so--it appears that the information and advice they are getting now is somehow lacking. Today there is so much relationship information on the internet, in books, from experts, and in courses. Yet family break ups and divorce are on the rise. Today there is more information and yet more problems. I am not knocking the various sources of information; I am just saying that something must be missing.

Where will we turn to find the kind of knowledge that will help us solve our problems once and for all, instead of just endlessly "working on our relationship?" Where will we find the kind of knowledge that will heal our relationships, restore our marriage, return the hearts of the children to the parents, and build a strong family?

Perhaps you have heard that long ago--when a young couple had marriage issues--a grandmother, a Dutch uncle, or an old and trusted friend would be called in.

That type of person had common sense, patience and understanding. They had both knowledge and know how. They had kindness, perhaps a twinkle in their eye.

They bore good will: they really and truly wanted the best to happen. They did not experiment with theories or approaches. Their guidance was solidly grounded in common sense, patience, and understanding.

That is what we need today. We need that type of know how, good will, and understanding.

The question is--where did the older and wiser person get their understanding? From a book or college course? No. It came from within. Understanding was the missing ingredient which tempered everything and showed them how to apply any knowledge they had gained.

Wouldn't it be nice if you could find understanding to deal with your marriage and family issues? If you had understanding yourself, then you could solve your own problems. Moreover, when you got information from external sources, your understanding and common sense would permit you to see which advice is good and which is not. If you had understanding, then you could listen to what others have to say and sift the wheat from the chaff.

You would know what to do with your knowledge and how to apply it with love and proper timing.

Sound too good to be true? Keep reading and I will show you the source of understanding, available to you now. I say that we can find this insight and deep understanding within when we learn to relate to our God-given intuition.

In the light of intuition, you would begin to see the reason why we squabble. Let me give you a few clues.

For example, you would begin to understand the mystery of the relationship between the sexes. It is an ancient and reoccurring cycle of ambition, rebellion, and failing. Just as in the story of the Garden of Eden, the woman is still used today to entice and support her modern day Adam to be ambitious.

When Adam looks to the woman and her guile for support instead of to principle, Paradise is lost and the family suffers. She feels used and he feels trapped and betrayed.

Without an understanding of the real dynamics in the man-woman relationship, people continue to hate and blame each other. Forgiveness is truly the answer. But in order to forgive, we must have insight into the deep dynamics behind all the squabbling we see in families.

We simply need to see, really see, where we are failing and why.

When you see that we humans are all in the same boat, you could be more forgiving toward your partner instead taking everything personally.

In order to do this, what we need is a very special kind of knowledge called understanding. You cannot get understanding from a book, even a religious book.

Understanding comes from intuition--what we know in our heart--when we look within and trust what we realize as our authority instead of looking to worldly experts. Intuition is first hand and alive.

External knowledge applied without understanding is second hand and lifeless. External knowledge is only useful when it awakens understanding and when it is applied with understanding.

Of course you can listen to what others have to say; just remember to run it by your gut instincts to see if it sits right with your intuition.

When it comes to marriage and family relationships, we need to understand why we fight. We need to understand our own inherent pride and see what is wrong with it. With understanding, we can also observe our own failings with compassion. We need to understand what other's true needs are. We need to understand that most of the time your loved ones are not being cruel on purpose. They are out of control.

The family is the bedrock of civilization. The relationship between the man and the woman within the institution of holy matrimony holds the key to happiness, prosperity, and domestic tranquility.

The family is the matrix in which the next generation comes forth, and it is the family which supports, nurtures and maintains the best of what it means to be a human.

Yet everywhere you look in the world--you see families boiling over with intrigue, betrayal, cruelty, suffering, and misery. Each and every couple starts off expecting to be happy. But something goes wrong. We need to understand why.

The kind of living knowledge I have in mind is found within. It is intuition. Some call it their highest instincts; some call it a gut level knowing. Some describe it as what they know in their heart. Even common sense is a basic form of this intuitive understanding. Whatever you call it--it is just what we need.

Look at it this way. Let's say a delicate situation arose between you and your partner or between you and your child. Suppose that out of disinterested love of what is right, you really and truly yearned with all your heart to know what to do. Let us suppose that you passed up on the quick angry response. You did not reach for a slogan, verse, or memorized one-size-fits-all fact to misapply. You heard but did not mindlessly follow the advice of other people. Instead, you waited and looked into your heart for wordless intuitive guidance.

Then whatever you did or did not say, or did or did not do, would be based in intuition, love, and common sense. It would spring from a deep and limitless source.

It would be rooted in rightness, love and principle. Its motivation would be selfless love, not expediency.

Your mate and your child would see the face of love: they would sense your quiet searching for what is right instead of seeking to win the argument or impatiently looking for a quick fix. The mere fact that they become aware of the presence of love already begins to restore right relationships.

Our families suffer for lack of this kind of knowledge. The one who is most to blame is the husband. It is his job to be the leader, the Moses, the David of the family.

It is his job to be a man of impeccable honor, courage, patience, understanding, kindness, forbearance, and graciousness and wisdom. Father is supposed to have understanding, and everything he does should be tinged with love and understanding.

There is no way that he can be the man he needs to be unless he finds an invisible bond with the Creator Within. He must be so grounded in principle and faith that there is no wavering, no failing, and no room for a lack of commitment to what is right.

He must be stronger than the world. But if he is woman centered, if women are the ground of his being and if his wife is his boss (or she lets him be the boss), then he will not be grounded in good. Instead he will be a beast man, violent or wimpy, grounded in the woman and beyond her in the serpent of old that tempted man through Eve.

My heart goes out to the decent women everywhere.

They are tempted to take charge because of the default of the man. They are tempted by his weakness to support and console his prideful ego. Men require it of women. And when she gains power because of his nothingness and growing weakness, she is then called upon to nag him to get him to function.

When he greedily goes for her love offerings, first with excitement then with resentment, he becomes enslaved.

And when he is enslaved by the temptation that he wanted from her, he is full of rage. The weak angry man goes off to another woman or to the bottle. The man who takes on her nature marries his work, money or becomes a seducer himself.

All the while, the children are suffering.

Men need to have a thorough knowledge of their own weakness.

They need to see just why they must not fail. They need to see why they must be principled and honorable.

Women need to see that the Adam and Eve story is recreated over and over again. They need to see that, yes, most men are weak and failures. But she must learn not to resent them for it. She must see her own role in tempting him and rising to the occasion of his need to gain power over him. She must see why she must not support him in his wrong, on the one hand, but must also not give him such a hard time that he doesn't have the space to find himself.

When you resent your husband, that resentment blocks understanding. In other words, when you become resentful or angry, you are disconnected from love. And love is what intuition has in it.

300

So now you know, dear reader, why understanding is the missing factor. It has love in it. Understanding is missing when couples resent each other; and it is missing when we try to apply external knowledge egotistically.

Perhaps a good starting point would be to just realize that your husband is just a man, and judging and nagging him will only stand in the way of his finding himself.

Men, you must see that you must not look to your wife to support your ego. Look within. You must look to no one except your Creator for the strength, wisdom and understanding that you do not now have, but will need if you are to be the kind of husband and father that your family needs.

Husbands and wives: regardless of what your situation is, begin right now to be more forgiving. Drop your grudges. If others are wrong, see their wrong, but don't hate them for it. Let go of judgment. Make it unimportant. You yourself become wrong through resentments and holding grudges. When you let go of judgment and blame, you will then be free to see what the real truth is. Do you see how intuition leads to understanding, and understanding to love?

- *38* -

Why Men Must Be Faithful and What to Do If You Have Cheated

Who was it who said: "Hell hath no fury like a woman scorned?" If only men understood just how devastating it is for a wife when a husband fails to be the noble man she had dreamt of and hoped for.

With the scandal of the infidelity of a famous professional athlete making headlines recently, what does a tough-minded Christian marriage coach have to say? Obviously we do not know all the facts, so there is no use speculating on this particular prominent person.

But because of the knowledge and skill I have acquired over the years, I can use the interest in marital relations the story has aroused to make some important points.

The first thing we can learn is this: a man must never fail. He must be principled and honorable. That is a father's role and husband's duty. When he fails the whole family suffers. I've been saying this for 20 years, and nothing has changed.

Secondly. I want to say that no one can make a man into a man. He must find it within himself.

It is the Father Spirit that our wives and children need. I will never forget something I once read. It was about the life of a sea captain who lived in the 1800's. It told how despite the fact that he was at sea for months at a time, his wife and his daughter felt secure and respected and loved him dearly.

They were happy and secure though he was thousands of miles away. He was a man of the highest honor and impeccable virtue. He was a noble, principled man doing his duty. He had the father spirit. They knew he would never fail them. And he never did. He had found an inner bond with his Creator.

If a man fails big time, his only hope is to realize his wrong, be sorry, apologize and then never fail again.

Maybe his wife will forgive him and maybe she won't. He must live the rest of his life honorably and with dignity. She may never forgive him. Even if she does not forgive him, he must continue in the marriage, do his duty and never look for sympathy. If she divorces him, he must live a principled and decent life. He must suffer in dignity--forever if necessary. He must not become bitter; he must become better.

Marriage was never meant to be a pleasure party. He must learn to be unselfish. It is his job to be there for his wife and kids. She will test him to see if he is sincere. She may test him and give him a hard time for years, decades even. He must never fail. Maybe one day she will see that he is sincere (not just pretending to have changed so as to keep the marriage perks). If nothing else, his nobility and quiet dignity will foster respect.

But if his apology is merely the crocodile tears of a wounded ego afraid of losing his perks, and not truly sincere, his duplicity will backfire. He must be sincere.

He must not seek to divorce his wife. If she divorces him and she gets the kids (which is most likely), then he must remain chaste and should not remarry, if possible.

He must live honorably and be available for the kids.

Divorce is a really big thing for kids. They will undoubtedly resent him for failing them. They may side with mom and hate him. He must never hate back. He must suffer in dignity, with good will. His goodwill and graciousness, his cheerfulness and chasteness, will at least not tempt them to resent him more.

Father stands in for God in the eyes of the child. That is why he must be principled, honorable, wise, thoughtful, kind, and he must stand for what is right (without anger). He must have no vices. A man cannot lecture about marijuana if he has a cigarette in his hand.

He cannot correct excessive socializing, for example, if he is surrounded by a bunch of phony friends. He must not be a wimp, but he should not be angry and violent either. He must search within for the patience and wisdom he needs and does not yet have.

As I have often said, most women have issues with their dad. He was not there for her, and she went out in the world looking for love. Chances are she had a bad experience or two with boyfriends who took advantage and did not really love her. Thus, when her husband fails her, it reminds her of all the previous men in her life who failed her.

When her husband fails, power goes to her. She is tempted to judge him and to hold him (and other men) in contempt. And she will probably hold his failing against him. Many women tend to have a memory a mile long when it comes to men's failures. All I can say is "serves him right."

Many men get married and expect it to be one big party. They have no idea how important husband and father are.

Their wife, on the other hand, has high expectations but fears he may turn out to be like other men. She may have some baggage from the past: unresolved issues beginning with her father who was not there for her.

She may also have been disappointed by other men, such as boy friends, who did not really love her.

When her husband fails in some way and she resents him, she tends to project her prior judgments on him.

He finds out that there is a lot more going on than just hearts and flowers and candy will fix. He discovers that he needs the wisdom of Solomon and the patience of Job which he does not have. What he should do at this point is realize his lack and seek his inner ground of being to find understanding.

Sadly, most men will err in how they go about seeking to repair the damage. Some whimper and beg their wife for forgiveness. These men are afraid of losing the comfy relationship they enjoyed. She may or may not accept her whimpering dog back. Either way she gains the power and ascends as his god. Though she may accept him back, she has no respect for him.

Other men will seek external guidance from ministers, support groups, accountability groups, counselors and other experts on how to be a better husband. Though the advice may be well intentioned and helpful, it is nevertheless second hand. It may validate what we know in our heart but should never substitute for it.

Without realizing it, he may become more externally based and dependent. What he needs is an independent means of support (his Creator within, actually). This is an inner thing, based on a re-found sincere commitment to principle, without any middleman involved. From this inner rapport will come intuition based understanding, as well as the patience, kindness, wisdom, commitment, and yes, courage to do what is right.

Some men seek support for their ego from other men, the bartender, alcohol, drugs or other temptations like gambling. But these supports (basically accepting him the way he is--prideful, selfish and unrepentant) just take the place of an ego supportive woman.

Remember, it was seeking support for his ego from his wife (or the other woman) that undermined him in the first place. Some men become married to their work or to money--these also take the place of the woman in supporting his ego.

As you can see, his troubles tested his commitment to principle and love for his family. Alas, his commitment and love were tested and found wanting. All that remains to be seen is whether or not he will be sincerely sorry and willing to change his ways or not. Without a true change of heart and commitment to principle, everything else is just window dressing.

As for the lady, I will just say that her emotional and spiritual well being depend on her being able to stop resenting and let go of her grudge against her husband (and all men). This does not mean that she has to like what he did or pretend nothing happened. It means seeing his failing, but not resenting him for it.

Just as at work a manager can deal with a difficult situation without resenting it, and can deal with a troublesome employee without resenting him, so we must learn to deal with personal situations without resentment.

Just as it is possible for a teacher or coach to see and patiently correct a student's mistakes (without resenting the student for it), while at the same time not supporting or condoning the mistakes--so can a wife see her husband's failing without supporting it on the one hand or condemning him on the other.

Men are always looking for a woman to mother and support his failings. This craving for (sexual) support for his failings can become exorbitant.

It is difficult for a woman to love her husband without supporting what is wrong with him. To the ladies I will just say: don't resent him. It is resentment that hurts us more than anything. Forgiveness is the answer. Again, I must say that forgiveness does not mean pretending nothing happened or going along with what happened. It means not resenting.

How wonderful it is to be married to a noble man.

Supporting him in this case is cooperating with and being a helpmate to his goodness. How much better this is than supporting and enabling what is wrong with another. Just remember that many men, though having failed as all men do, nevertheless begin to wake up and learn to be unselfish. Such men become more fatherly and one day transcend their former weaknesses.

If there is any goodness in him, there is hope that he might yet become the man you want him to be. If so, your continued resentment of him is just another pressure that makes it hard for him to function. By backing off a little and letting go of resentment, you give him the space to find himself.

When a woman resents her husband, she tends to then feel guilty (for the resentment and judgment). She then blames herself and seeks to "be a better wife" to make up for the guilt. Watch out for this trap. Self blame and guilt result from the resentment and judgment. Let go of resentment, and you will be able to honestly assess what is going on without guilt.

Of course, my fondest desire would be reconciliation and forgiveness, with both sides realizing their role in the situation. Alas, reconciliation and true forgiveness do not usually happen, but there is always hope. And yes, I understand that if the man is a terrible cad, a separation may be the best and safest way to go. The main thing is watch out for resentment. Let it go. Be there for the kids. Live on in dignity and graciousness.

Therefore, dear ladies, forgive your husband.

Men--although you have failed, your past selfishness and lack of understanding may yet result in a happy ending if your suffering moves you to repentance and change of heart, leading to the hope of repair and reconciliation. Drop resentment, and let love come through.

- 39 -

The Strong Family— Ten Lessons in Faithfulness

Sure, money and career are important. But at the end of the day, family is more important. Single persons can devote themselves to career, but when a family forms, everything changes. Integrity and healthy relationships become the keys to true success. That's why when a partner is unfaithful, it is usually devastating to all the other family members.

Together let's ponder the disappointment and betrayal people feel when a partner cheats. Maybe we can remember to appreciate our own family just a little more. Perhaps we can even take away a lesson or two that will help us to be better partners and parents.

Lesson one. Honor your commitments and do your duty. Someone is counting on you. In fact, if you step outside the bounds of marriage, the message to your wife and kids is: dad does not love us. I know this is a hard teaching, but hear me out.

Isn't it true that when a well known person (you had respected) is discovered cheating, you feel disappointment at some deep unplumbed level? If so, you are getting a small dose of what the partner and kids feel when something like this happens to the family.

You husbands and dads--I hope you see why you must never fail, because of the effect it has on others.

For example, if you feel a little let down by unfaithful sports heroes, you're not alone. Plenty of people feel hurt and betrayed. I understand. Thank goodness I have found a solid spiritual base for my life.

Nevertheless, even I occasionally feel a little disappointment when someone I had looked up to lets me down. Let it be a reminder to us all to do our duty. Someone is counting on us.

Lesson two. Moms and dads, you are the first role models in your kids' lives. Don't let them down. In fact, if you have any public visibility at all, people will identify with you. Any appearance of impropriety disappoints and disillusions them. Your kids identify with you too.

No wonder many of us are disappointed when a sports hero, for example, does something wrong. We took it for granted that what our sports coaches always told us was true: that sports build character. We thought that we could safely identify with someone and look up to someone as a role model without being embarrassed or let down.

But dads, here is the good news. The failings of others will not bother your kids if *you* do not fail them or let them down.

Lesson three. I have always heard that integrity is important. I heard that the word "integrity" came from the Latin word meaning "whole or undivided." But I never really understood the term. Now I see that many people who are unfaithful have compartmentalized their lives. They are not whole, they are divided.

Now I see that integrity means wholeness. That's one thing most of us love and respect about our moms.

Mom is always mom. You get the whole Mom all the time. She may not be perfect, but she has integrity.

What can you say about a man who has a secret life? It is not a good thing. A man of character is whole. He is always the same. He is the same through and through, and he has no secret life.

Lesson four. Be a champ. Dad, your wife and kids are likely to put you on a pedestal. They want to look up to you. They want to respect you. They want to trust you.

You are more than just a role model to them--you stand for something very special.

Watching the scandal stories, you can see with your own eyes how quickly a person can go from being a champ to a chump. Don't let it happen to you.

Now let me address myself to the ladies and kids (after all, even we grown-ups are adult children of our parents).

Lesson five. Maybe your dad is not such a bad guy after all. Is he home every night? Is he true to your mom? Then no matter how little money he makes--in the arena of fidelity, he is a bigger man than any successful person who cheats on his wife.

Lesson six. Be grateful for a husband who goes to work, comes home, watches television and works in the garage. If he is basically a good guy, don't give him such a hard time. Okay, he's not perfect. But don't we always say "No one is perfect?"

Lesson seven. Many men are far more decent than you realize. Many dads appear nerdy and simple because they don't do a lot of "cool" things. Instead, they talk about work and the weather. They read the paper and watch the news. They tend to fall asleep on

311

the couch (after a hard day's work). Therefore, some of us assume that dad is boring.

Could it be that dad is eschewing the exciting life in order to be there for his family? In other words, maybe he is living a quiet and dull life not because he has to but because he has chosen to. Maybe he is sacrificing selfish pleasure for the sake of his wife and kids.

Lesson eight. Dad may not be dumb. Dads sometimes appear dumb because they don't say much.

Could it be that he is exercising patience and self control? Could it be that he sees things that trouble him, but holds his tongue? Could it be that he is sometimes hurt, but he says nothing because he does not want to return the hurt? Could it be that his thoughts and love are too profound for him to easily put in words?

Lesson nine. Cherish and appreciate your family's love. Men, have you ever received a mug or a greeting card from your child that says something like: "My dad is my hero?" Women, have you ever received a card that says "to the world's greatest mom?" If you have, cherish it, for it is worth more than any degree, title, or trophy the world has to offer. Make sure you are worthy of it.

Gentlemen, now that you have been reminded of what it is like to be betrayed and disappointed by someone, don't mess up. Put a picture of your wife and kids on your desk at work. Wear your wedding ring at all times (this applies to you wives too). When you travel, carry a big picture of your wife and kids with you and place it in plain sight in every hotel room you stay in.

Lesson ten. Get married. I know this is a little controversial. But I say it after thirty years of teaching and counseling. If you and your partner are just living together, may I suggest you consider tying the knot and making it formal?

Never mind what everyone says about it "just being a piece of paper" and so on. Marriage is not casual (even if you think it is). The formality of wedding vows before a justice of the peace or minister, witnessed by others, means commitment and fidelity. It says that you really mean it. If you are unwilling to sign on the dotted line and say "I do," it means you are not 100% committed. It has the appearance of impropriety.

Even if you are 99% committed, you can be sure that your partner is aware of the 1%. Trust me.

After you are married, just for fun, frequently wear a tee shirt that says: "Sorry, I'm already taken."

- *40* -

Restoring Order in the Home and Nation via a Change of Heart

Who can forget the wonderful movie Robin Hood starring the dashing handsome Errol Flynn and the beautiful Olivia DeHavilland? While the good King Richard the Lion Hearted is out of the Country, the rotten Sheriff of Nottingham and his cohorts are up to no good.

Robin, with a love for his country, honor, courage, and a keen sense of fairness, fights against injustice and risks his life to do good.

Robin has no respect for wrong authorities. He thumbs his nose at them and gives them a hard time.

When King Richard the Lion Hearted returns from afar, he at first travels incognito because of the personal danger to him and so he can quietly discover what is happening in his kingdom. He wears a monk's outfit with a hood so that no one will recognize him.

Through fate, Robin meets up with the King in the forest without knowing who he is. When the King takes off his monkish robe to reveal his kingly attire, Robin drops to one knee and says: "My Lord."

Robin Hood, a mighty man of valor, would bow his knee to no man except before the one who is truly respectable, the Good King Richard the Lion Hearted.

And of course, the beautiful Olivia DeHavilland did not want to marry the terrible person they had in mind for her. She liked Robin because he was courageous and noble. She would only give her hand in marriage to the one who was truly worthy.

So it is in life. Everywhere there are weak and wrong authorities. Some are half way decent but not strong enough. Others are scoundrels. Many are simply selfish or misguided.

Where is the noble person we can truly respect?

Fortunately, there are such noble men and women around. Perhaps you are destined to become one of them. But in order to become the person of wisdom, grace, and courage, you must travel a special road of discovery. And upon this road you will learn to give up what has blocked you from developing to your full potential.

It has been faithlessness, selfishness, resentment and judgment that separated you from your own ground of being. Once separated you could only compensate from the outside. Knowledge, popularity, and setting goals made you more and more like the ones who tempted you to resent them in the first place.

How to get back? Well, there is a protocol involved.

Our Creator is the Good King, and we have all betrayed Him and sold ourselves down the river for a few trinkets, perks or popularity.

Then when conscience, our closest link to God, made us aware we had done something wrong, we ran from conscience into distractions, emotions, and imagination.

But if you could become still and permit your conscience to dawn on you, it would again begin to make you aware of what it has been trying to wordlessly tell you all along.

And if instead of reaching away to some distraction, you let conscience overwhelm, you might begin to experience a quiet sorrow, a sense of helpless regret when you see something wrong about yourself.

The first thing your conscience might make you aware of is that you hated your dad or resented your mom. Whatever it is, were you to quietly bear the pain of seeing the truth, the shaming and redeeming regret would signal a capitulation to God and His right Way.

Just as Robin Hood submits to the one person he can respect, so your soul can submit to the wordless Truth.

You see the Truth does not lie when it shows you your wrong.

And it, being true and honorable, stern and yet kind, is respectable.

It is positively good for your soul to honor the truth.

And it is the beginning of salvation when your soul is willing to admit it is wrong in the Light of Truth.

It says in the Bible that God does not despise a contrite heart. Repentance is the first life-giving emotion. It reconciles you to God Who sends His Light of Truth.

And a most wonderful thing happens. Even amidst the tears, there is a quiet gladness.

It is a sad glad. You are sad to see your wrong but glad that the Truth is there showing you. And when the brief pain is over, joy returns. The world will be sweeter. Not because I say so, but because that is the way it will be when the soul is touched by Truth and is receptive.